Previous Books by Rabbi Berel Wein:

TRIUMPH OF SURVIVAL
The Story of the Jews in the Modern Era 1648–2000

HERALDS OF DESTINY
The Story of the Jews in the Medieval Era 750–1648

ECHOES OF GLORY
The Story of the Jews in the Classical Era 350 BCE–750 CE

FAITH AND FATE
The Story of the Jews in the Twentieth Century

PESACH HAGADAH
Notes and Comments on the Seder Night

PIRKEI AVOS—The Ethics of the Fathers
Notes and Comments to the Book of Jewish Values

SECOND THOUGHTS

BUY GREEN BANANAS

TENDING THE VINEYARD
The Life and Vicissitudes of Being a Rabbi

LIVING JEWISH
A Guide to Jewish Life

RABBI BEREL WEIN

The Oral Law of Sinai

An Illustrated History of the Mishnah

An Arthur Kurzweil Book

JOSSEY-BASS
A Wiley Imprint
www.josseybass.com

Copyright © 2008 by John Wiley & Sons, Inc. All rights reserved.

Published by Jossey-Bass
A Wiley Imprint
989 Market Street, San Francisco, CA 94103-1741—www.josseybass.com

Graphic Design: Ben Gasner Studio

No part of this publication may be reproduced, stored in a retrieval system, or transmitted in any form or by any means, electronic, mechanical, photocopying, recording, scanning, or otherwise, except as permitted under Section 107 or 108 of the 1976 United States Copyright Act, without either the prior written permission of the publisher, or authorization through payment of the appropriate per-copy fee to the Copyright Clearance Center, Inc., 222 Rosewood Drive, Danvers, MA 01923, 978-750-8400, fax 978-646-8600, or on the Web at www.copyright.com. Requests to the publisher for permission should be addressed to the Permissions Department, John Wiley & Sons, Inc., 111 River Street, Hoboken, NJ 07030, 201-748-6011, fax 201-748-6008, or online at www.wiley.com/go/permissions.

Readers should be aware that Internet Web sites offered as citations and/or sources for further information may have changed or disappeared between the time this was written and when it is read.

Limit of Liability/Disclaimer of Warranty: While the publisher and author have used their best efforts in preparing this book, they make no representations or warranties with respect to the accuracy or completeness of the contents of this book and specifically disclaim any implied warranties of merchantability or fitness for a particular purpose. No warranty may be created or extended by sales representatives or written sales materials. The advice and strategies contained herein may not be suitable for your situation. You should consult with a professional where appropriate. Neither the publisher nor author shall be liable for any loss of profit or any other commercial damages, including but not limited to special, incidental, consequential, or other damages.

Jossey-Bass books and products are available through most bookstores. To contact Jossey-Bass directly call our Customer Care Department within the U.S. at 800-956-7739, outside the U.S. at 317-572-3986, or fax 317-572-4002.

Jossey-Bass also publishes its books in a variety of electronic formats. Some content that appears in print may not be available in electronic books.
Credits appear on p. 189-190

Library of Congress Cataloging-in-Publication Data
Wein, Berel.
   The oral law of Sinai : an illustrated history of the Mishnah / Berel Wein.
   p. cm.
   "An Arthur Kurzweil Book."
   "A Wiley Imprint."
   Includes bibliographical references and index.
   ISBN 978-0-470-19755-4 (cloth)
1. Mishnah—History. 2. Mishnah—Criticism, interpretation, etc.
3. Judaism—History—Talmudic period, 10-425. 4. Legends, Jewish. I. Title.
   BM497.85.W45 2008
   296.1'23067—dc22
                                   2007050410

Printed in the United States of America
FIRST EDITION
HB Printing   10 9 8 7 6 5 4 3 2 1

Table of Contents

Acknowledgments — XI
In the Beginning — 1

I. From Ezra to Hillel and Shammai
c. 350 BCE – 30 BCE

Ezra	11
Shimon HaTzaddik	15
The *Zugos*	19
Yosi ben Yoezer and Yosi ben Yochanan	20
Yehoshua ben Prachyah and Nitai HaArbeli	23
Yehudah ben Tabai and Shimon ben Shatach	25
Shmaya and Avtalyon	30
Hillel and Shammai	32

II. Raban Shimon ben Hillel to Rabi Akiva
c. 30 BCE – 200 CE

Transmitting Tradition	45
Raban Shimon ben Hillel	46

Raban Gamliel I (The Elder)	47
Colleagues of Raban Gamliel I	51
Shmuel HaKatan	51
Akavya ben Mehalalel	52
Rabi Chanina (Chananya) Sgan HaKohanim	52
Rabi Eliezer ben Yaakov I	53
Raban Shimon ben Gamliel I	55
Raban Yochanan ben Zakai	58
Rabi Eliezer ben Hyrkanos and Rabi Yehoshua ben Chananya	70
The Heavy Hand of Rome	83
Rabi Akiva	91

Rabi Meir to Rabi Yehudah HaNasi
c. 140 CE – 200 CE

The End of an Era	103
Rabi Meir	108
Raban Shimon ben Gamliel II	117
Rabi Yehudah HaNasi	120
Rabi Chiya	126
The Writing of the Mishnah	129

Appendices

Shishah Sidrei Mishnah	146
Tannaim Timeline	148
Notes	151
Glossary	175
About the Author	181
Index	183
Photo Credits	189

*In memory of
my dear and beloved friends,
Lillian and Leslie Hirtz,
whose exemplary lives and behavior
made every moment of their lives
and the lives of their children and
grandchildren — in the words
of the Mishnah — "A Time for God."*

Acknowledgments

I am indebted to many for their helping me in being able to see this book come to print and distribution. I thank my dear friends, Rabbi Yehonosan and Rochelle Hirtz, Dr. Henry and Susie Zupnick and Menachem and Marjorie Adler for their moral and financial support that enabled this book to be designed and set. It was their help that provided the impetus for the book project to become real. My gratitude to the Green family in all of their generations and their Darchei Noam Foundation is as unlimited as their friendship and support of me has been over the years. Without their generosity and encouragement, this book would probably have remained merely a good idea whose time somehow had not come. They helped raise me from a moment of personal despair and challenged me to keep on going. And they did so in the classy, gentle and firm way that is the hallmark of their relationships with others. My colleagues at Destiny Foundation, Elaine Gilbert and Miriam Cubac, were also of inestimable help to me in seeing this book through to its final completion.

On the technical end of whipping this book into shape my thanks and deepest gratitude go to Charlotte Friedland, the editor par supreme. Her painstaking review of the manuscript uncovered many weaknesses and prevented much slipshod language or undocumented research to enter the book. Ben Gasner is one of the world's great book designers and graphic artists. The layout, illustrations and appearance of this book testify to his genius and talent in this area. His entire staff in his Jerusalem workshop excelled in every facet of skill and professionalism. Dr. Allison Kupietzky researched and obtained the photographs and illustrations that are such an important part of the book. The publisher of this book, Jossey Bass, has done nobly as usual in producing and distributing this book. I am indebted to Alan Rinzler who shepherded this project to its completion with patience, skill and good humor.

I thank my friend Peter Steinlauf for getting me to contact Margy-Ruth Davis who kindly put me in touch with Arthur Kurzweil who then in turn put me in touch with Alan Rinzler. My thanks go to Moishe and Josselyn Halibard for their meticulous proofreading and incisive spelling and organizational suggestions. I am also grateful to Leah Ben-Avraham for her skilled layout and talents in graphic arts. Producing a book is a complicated matter and there are always many people involved. I thank them all for their help and friendship.

Finally my thanks go to my family and the members of my congregation here in Jerusalem who stood by me while this book was being written and produced. There are no adequate words to convey my appreciation to them and my love for them. May the Lord of Israel and of all of humanity bless them and may the merit of the great people of the Mishnah and the Talmud who appear in this book stand us all in good stead accompanied by faith and blessings.

*To my beloved friends,
Pinky and Libby
and all of their family
with deep appreciation
and affection.*

Author's Note

In the Mishnah text itself the title *Rabi* is usually used before the full name of the scholars of the Mishnah, though sometimes the title *Rabbi* is also properly used. The title and name *Rabi* is always used for Rabi Yehuda HaNasi, and he is called just plain *Rabi* throughout the Mishnah. I have attempted to adhere to the titles used in the Mishnah regarding each of the scholars, though in reality the titles *Rabbi* and *Rabi* are really interchangeable. I pray that you will not find this confusing and realize that these are not typographical errors but rather an attempt to be as faithful as possible to the language and ideas of the Mishnah itself.

In the Beginning

here is no intellectual work known to the human world that is even similar to the Mishnah and its companion work, the Talmud. The Talmud is a law book, a faithful transmission of the Oral Law of Sinai to all later generations of Jews. It is a book of ethical principles and moral values. It is a book of legends and stories, and also of psychological and historical observations. It discusses medicine, pharmacology, dreams, botany, astronomy and mathematics, as well as human and animal biology. It is a detailed, painstaking commentary to the Written Law of the Torah, based on rigorous logic, scrupulous scrutiny of the biblical texts, and an unremitting search for truth.

It does not debate matters of faith—it is faith itself. It discovers God and His Torah in every nook and cranny of human existence and there is nothing about life, humans, nature, spirituality or physicality that is a taboo subject. All is Torah; all is holiness.

Replete with humor, irony, pathos, soaring optimism and cold-hearted realism, its mode—and drama—emerge from the give and take of intensive scholarly debate and unending questioning, probing and hypothesizing.

It is a joy to study, but it is not entertaining. The Talmud is maddeningly difficult and sometimes determinedly abstruse. It makes no concessions, not in language nor intellect, to its students. Its reasoning and methods are rigorous. Every word, every sentence and phrase is a new challenge. The text has very little punctuation, and its long and complicated run-on sentences can go for pages on end. It demands a seriousness of purpose, a willingness to commit time and sweat to its study, before it will give up its secrets and insights.

In reality, the Talmud is two separate books comprising the Oral Law. The first is the Mishnah, the subject of this book. Written circa third century BCE, its language is classical, post-biblical Hebrew. It is studied as a subject in and of itself. However, the Talmud, also known as Gemara, is written in the Aramaic of third to fifth century Babylonian Jewry. Every page of the Talmud includes the passage of Mishnah upon which its discussion is based, as well as later teachings and commentary.

A key feature of both the Mishnah and the Talmud is that they can never be understood from the outside. As a unique work with its own method of reasoning, it can be known only from the inside—from the Talmud itself! So, the obvious question is, where does one begin? One must struggle to get into the heart of the Talmud, for only by reaching its heart can one hope to penetrate the intricacies of its mental processes and appreciate the magic of its logic. Since the Talmud can only be known from inside, intellect alone (though certainly necessary) is insufficient to master it. Minds can speak to minds, but only hearts can speak to hearts.

Page from Talmud Bavli, Masechet Megila, Venice, 1523 (Jewish National & University Library)

The Talmud is a book of godly personalities and deep insight into the human condition and the world. It is a book of love, of compassion, of striving spirituality and also of withering candor. It is a book for the masses, but it is again a book only for the few. It has simple wisdom on its surface and majestic mystery in its depth.

It is the book of love between Jews and Jews, between generations and generations, between the people and the God of Israel. Therefore, one who measures the Talmud by the yardstick of facts, laws, and discussions alone makes a fundamental error, for that is a very narrow, and even unjust, view of this monumental work.

For the triumph of the Talmud and its personalities against its enemies, both within and without the Jewish people, was based upon its hidden greatness and human warmth, not only on its soaring intellect and wise interpretations of Jewish law. The creators of the Mishnah and Talmud are the worthy successors to the prophets of Israel in their vision, their fire and passion, their unsparing honesty, their love for the people and God of Israel; and most of all, in their almost unrealistic yet unquenchable optimism. Theirs is the unshakable faith in the Torah and mission of Israel that sustained generations of Jews for centuries.

But perhaps the greatest contribution of the Oral Law—and of the Mishnah and Talmud that now represents that Oral Law—is found in the words of Midrash itself:

> *"I [the Lord] do not wish to grant them the Oral Law in writing because I know that the nations of the world will rule over the Jews and take it away from them. Thus, the written Bible I give them [now] in writing, while the Mishnah, Talmud and Aggadah I grant to them orally, for when the nations of the world will in the future subjugate Israel, the Jews will still be able to be separate from them ... for they [the words of the Oral Law] are what will separate the Jewish people from being assimilated and lost into the general society"* (Midrash Rabah Shmos, chapter 47, section one).

Thus, even though the entire Torah, both Written and Oral, is from Sinai, the portion of Torah that is the Oral Law remains solely in Jewish possession, unlike the written Bible that has been co-opted by other faiths. In this way, the Oral Law has contributed significantly to the survival of the Jews as a unique and vital people. The Oral Law can be seen as the dividing line between Israel and the nations of the world. The Written Law, the Bible, can be characterized as universal: the Oral Law, as represented in the Mishnah and Talmud, as particular. The genius of incorporating both of these ideas and balancing them harmoniously within Judaism is testimony to the strength and truth of the Jewish faith.

The Oral Law is built upon the Written Torah. Though it was a product of centuries of study, writing, editing and endless review, Judaism posits that the Oral Law—its structure, mechanisms, and its interpretations of the Written Torah—stems from the Divinity of the Revelation at Sinai. Every subject in the Talmud begins with the question: "Where in the Written Torah [in the text itself] do we find the basis for this discussion?"

However, the development, scholarship and popularization of the Oral Law were accomplished by people. And it is these people who lie at the heart of the Mishnah and Talmud. These great human beings accelerated this process of developing the Oral Law after the end of the period of prophecy in Jewish history, during the era of Ezra and the Men of the Great Assembly (approximately 350-300 BCE). In fact, the development of the Oral Law as the main spiritual and intellectual basis of Judaism from the time of Ezra onwards should be seen as the replacement for the now absent gift of prophecy which had previously sustained the nation of Israel from the time of Moses till Ezra. Until the final redaction of the Babylonian Talmud (approximately 450 CE), this process of interpretation and decision-making, stretching over almost a millennia in time, continued unabated.

Neither the destruction of the Second Temple (70 CE) nor the failure of the later Bar Kochba rebellion (c. 132 CE) stopped the process of refining and studying the Oral Law. Through Greek and Roman persecution and the challenges of pagan culture, even through the later rise of Christianity and its open hostility towards Jews and Judaism, the work of the noble scholars of the Mishnah and Talmud continued. Their academies of learning flourished, first in the Land of Israel and then in Babylonia.

Who were these great men? What do we know of their lives and fortunes? How were they able to ignore the damaging winds that swirled around them and remain focused on the development of the Oral Law? Like the Talmud itself, their life stories are not found in outside sources. They are found only in the Mishnah, the Talmud and in attendant works of Torah scholarship—Midrash, Tosefta, Targum, etc. As stated above, the only way to understand the Talmud is through its heart, and these transcendent individuals are its very heart. It is therefore through the lives of these people that the story of the development of the Mishnah and Talmud will be told. That is why I believe that this book can be a boon to all students of the Mishnah and Talmud, veteran and novice, skilled and struggling.

The study of Mishnah and Talmud has been enhanced and popularized by its relatively recent availability in English. Special commendation is due to the Mesorah Heritage Foundation that has supported the publication of the monumental Artscroll edition of the Talmud with its English elucidation. However, to the best of my knowledge, a popular review of the lives and personalities of the creators of the Mishnah and Talmud has not yet been made available to the wider English-speaking public. There are some wonderful works on this subject in Hebrew. Chief among them are those of Eliezer Shteinman, Avraham Naftal, Aharon Heiman, Yisrael Konovitz, Chaim Koolitz, Yitzchak Isaac Halevi, Reuven Margoliyus and Zev Yavetz. Mosad Harav Kook in Jerusalem has published a multi-volume series in Hebrew anthologizing the sayings and teachings of many of the individual scholars of the Mishnah and Talmud. I have availed myself liberally of these works in my endeavor to portray the lives of the masters of the Talmud for the English-speaking public. I humbly acknowledge my debt to the scholarship and intellectual prowess of these above named scholars, and to other unnamed ones as well. But as this book will continually show, primarily I have allowed the

Cylinder by Cyrus documenting his capture of Babylon and the return of captured people in Babylon to their homelands, Babylon, circa 539-530 BCE (The British Museum)

Mishnah and Talmud itself to speak about its creators and authors. Therefore, this book is more a work of organization and compilation than of original creative scholarship.

The chapters of this book are arranged in an approximate chronological order. Naturally, the story of some of the people discussed will cover pages, while others will only fill a few sentences. This distinction is not a judgment as to the relative importance of the subjects involved, but rather a reflection of the amount of material present in the pages of the Mishnah and Talmud regarding that particular personage. Many remarkable people preferred to remain hidden in the history of that time (and of later times as well) and the Mishnah and Talmud apparently were willing to accommodate those wishes. In any event, this work is not an encyclopedia nor is it meant to be all encompassing in its scope. My goal is to reveal the heart of the Oral Law and illuminate the lives of the creators of these great books upon which the Jewish nation has built its society and lifestyle for the past fifteen centuries.

Detail from a wall plaque for the Remembrance of Jerusalem by Zalman Zweig, circa 1910 (The Gross Family Collection, Israel)

In this volume regarding the Mishnah, we will cover two main periods of Jewish history. The first historical period deals with the people of the Great Assembly and the *Zugos*—the "pairs"—who were the transmitters of the Oral Law from the time of Ezra to the time of Hillel and Shammai. This period covers slightly more than 300 years. Hillel rose to prominence in the year 30 BCE and he and his colleague, Shammai, created two great schools of learning that focused on the development of the Oral Law: they are known as Beis Hillel and Beis Shammai.

This leads us to the second period of history which the book describes: that of the people and times of the Tannaim, the scholars who created, developed and eventually edited and published the Mishnah. This process took place over 250 years, till the beginning of the third century CE.

A second volume hopefully will detail the lives and times of the Amoraim, the people who, in studying and analyzing the Mishnah, created the Babylonian and Jerusalem Talmud, which absorbed the Mishnah into its corpus. The period of time involved in completing this endeavor was approximately 250 years, ending in the middle decades of the fifth century CE. The final editing of the Talmud, in the form that we have it today was accomplished by the Savoraim—the "explainers"—who completed their redaction of the Talmud by the beginning of the seventh century CE.

Of course, this book is unable to detail the lives of the many hundreds, if not thousands, of people involved in producing this massive and monumental work of holy scholarship. In fact, as I have mentioned earlier, many of these extraordinary people have successfully retained their anonymity throughout time. I have therefore chosen the key people, as the Mishnah itself lists them, as the subjects of this book.

I pray that in some way I do justice to their lives and achievements. I am ever mindful of the assessment of the rabbis of the Talmud: "If the people of the previous generations were angels, then we may consider ourselves to be humans. But if they were only humans, then we are only as donkeys…" (Shabbos 112b). I have therefore stayed away from character judgments and any personal opinions of mine. I am satisfied to let the Mishnah and Talmud themselves tell the story of those who fashioned it so carefully and lovingly.

SECTION 1

FROM EZRA TO HILLEL AND SHAMMAI

C. 350 BCE - 30 BCE

THE ORAL LAW OF SINAI

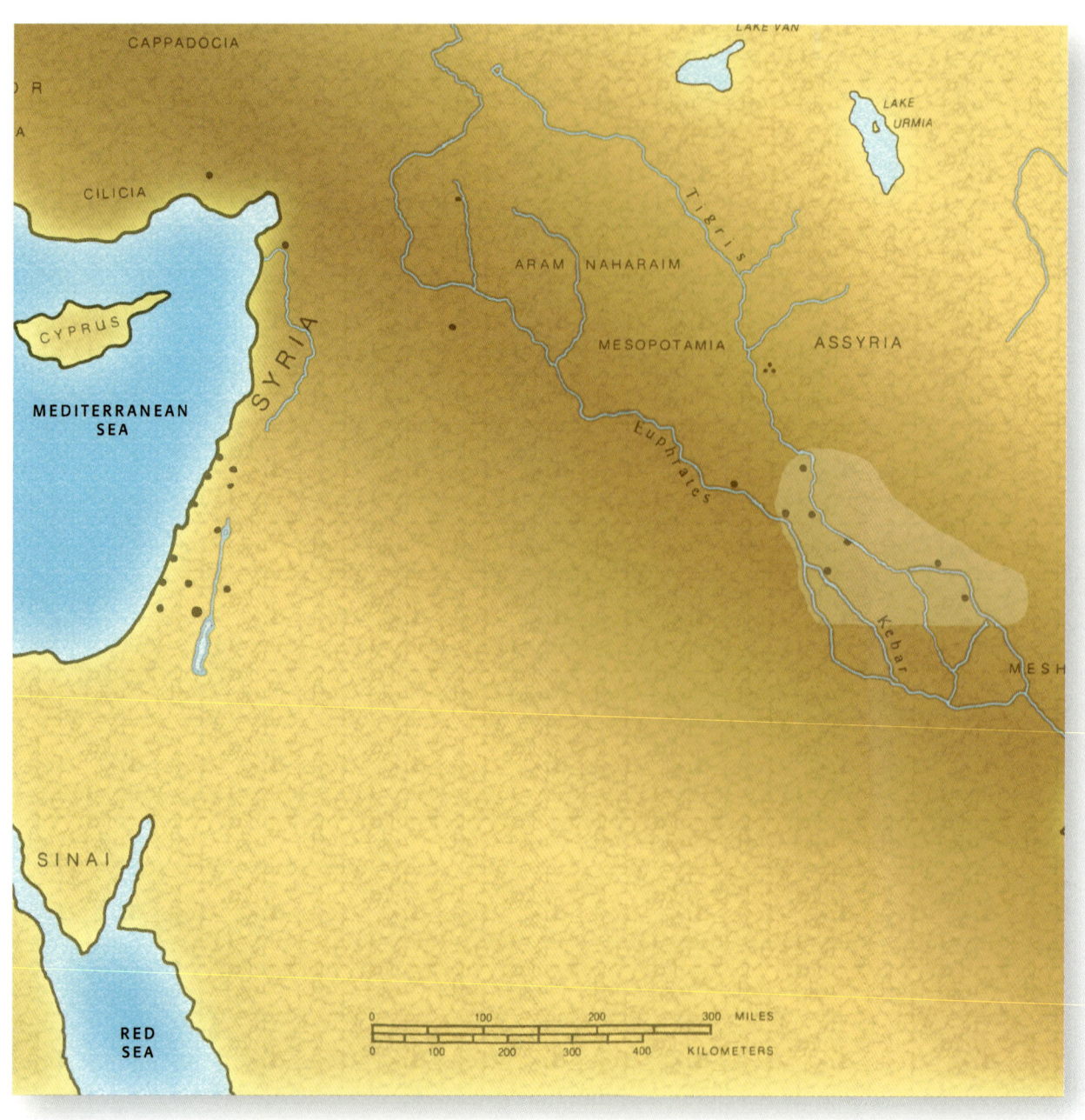

Ezra

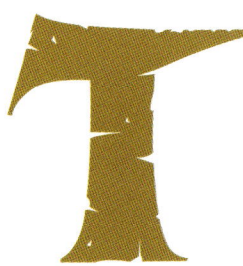The vast majority of Jews in Babylonia refused to heed Ezra's call to return to their homeland in the Land of Israel. Those who did return to Jerusalem from Babylonian exile had to face a devastating array of physical and spiritual problems: armed conflict with the Samaritans and their non-Jewish allies for control of territory, exacerbated by the fact that the defensive wall around Jerusalem was in ruins; rampant Jewish assimilation and intermarriage; open desecration of the Sabbath; and a volatile and oftentimes hostile Persian governing authority.

One would think that in the face of such a dangerous, depressing, and enervating series of problems, there would be scant attention paid to the great task of developing and popularizing the Oral Law. However, Ezra, Nechemiah, Zerubavel, Chaggai, Zechariah, Malachi (there is an opinion in the Talmud that identifies Malachi with Ezra himself), Mordechai and the other original 120 members of the *Knesses HaGedolah*—the Great Assembly—thought otherwise. They knew that without a strong spiritual Torah atmosphere in Israel, all of the possible solutions to these pressing problems ultimately would prove inadequate. That Torah atmosphere, which would have to be developed in the waning last days of prophecy within Israel, could be supplied only by the intensification of study and development of the Oral Law.

And that is exactly what happened. Ezra was a kohein—a member of the priestly tribe of Israel, a direct descendant of Aaron, the

EZRA
c. 350 BCE
Teacher
• Baruch Ben Neriyah
Colleagues
• Nechemiah
• Zerubavel
• Chaggai
• Zechariah
• Malachi
• Mordechai
• Yehoshua ben Yehotzadak Kohein Gadol
Students
• The Men of the Great Assembly
Relatives
• Nephew: Yehoshua ben Yehotzadak, Kohein Gadol

THE ORAL LAW OF SINAI

first High Priest, and he became the chief architect of the development of the Oral Law. There would be many contractors and builders, workers and finishers who would follow him in erecting this greatest of spiritual structures in Jewish history. But it was Ezra who supplied the vision and the impetus for the development of the Oral Law. He was a scribe and a disciple of Baruch ben Neriyah, the "secretary" of the prophet Jeremiah. Baruch originally followed Jeremiah into exile in Egypt, but later joined the majority of his brethren in Babylonia. As long as Baruch was still alive, Ezra did not leave him to return to the Land of Israel.[1] Ezra's greatness in Torah was so obvious that the rabbis said regarding him: "The Torah could have been given to Israel by Ezra if it were not that Moses preceded him."[2]

Jeremiah's Lamentations by Marc Chagall, 1887-1985. Original double sided lithograph from Verve La Bible, 1956

Gentle of character but iron in will, Ezra established the basic religious and political infrastructure of the nascent Jewish commonwealth. Aside from serving as the temporal and religious leader of the returning Jewish exiles, Ezra was the most likely candidate to be *Kohein Gadol*—High Priest—of the newly built Holy Temple, but in his modesty, he deferred to Yehoshua ben Yehotzadok, whose immediate ancestors had served in that position in First Temple times. To make sure that Yehoshua would be assured of the position, Ezra postponed coming to Jerusalem until after Yehoshua had already been installed as *Kohein Gadol*. For this gesture alone, the rabbis characterized Ezra as "*ish tzadik*"—a man of righteousness.[3]

However, implicit in Ezra's decision was also the reluctance of the rabbis throughout the ages to place too much power in the hands of one person, no matter how righteous and talented that one person may be. According to tradition, Ezra was the uncle of Yehoshua, the High Priest. Ezra was reluctant to take too much power for himself, and his own children never served in high office. However, a descendant of his in the tenth generation after him, Rabi Elazar ben Azaryah, did serve as the *Nasi* of the Sanhedrin in the second century CE.[4]

The central accomplishment of Ezra—and perhaps the greatest eulogy one could have—was expressed in Avos D'Rabi Nosson: "He focused his heart to understand and develop the Torah of God, and to accomplish the observance of the Torah, and then to teach Israel Torah law and justice."[5]

> "And I have strengthened myself as the hand of God has been upon me and I have gathered the leaders of Israel to go up with me (to the Land of Israel)."
> *Ezra*

During the time of Ezra, the work of the Great Assembly was of paramount importance. This group developed the infrastructure that would later grow into the Talmud. They did not *create* the Oral Law. That was done on Sinai through Moses. During the period of the First Temple, there already had existed *megillos*—handwritten notes and scrolls—that recorded the *halachah* (law) as developed by the Oral Law. In keeping with the mandate that the Oral Law was to be taught publicly only orally, with the necessary exposition of it by the person teaching it to his students, these *megillos* were never made public.[6] However, there was never a prohibition against private individuals writing notes and *megillos* regarding the Oral Law for their own personal use. It was the distribution and public use of these *megillos* that was forbidden.[7]

Graffito of a menorah, incense altar and shewbread table, Jewish Quarter of the Old City, Jerusalem. Herodian period, 1st century BCE (Collection of the Israel Antiquities Authority)

Until the time of the Hasmoneans, there is no record of disputes in *halachah* in Jewish legal sources. All of the legal and interpretative disputes, differing opinions of the various Torah scholars, and

THE ORAL LAW OF SINAI

conflicting traditions amongst the Jewish people were settled in a definitive fashion by the Sanhedrin in every generation. It is only in later centuries, when the power of the Sanhedrin weakened—and definitive decisions thus were more difficult to create and achieve universal acceptance—that differing opinions regarding particular *halachos* of the Oral Law became common. These differences were then dutifully recorded and preserved in the Mishnah proper. As long as the men of the Great Assembly, their students and their students' students (the *Sheyarei Knesses HaGedolah*)—remnants of the Great Assembly)[8]—were still alive and functioning, all matters of *halachah* were settled and defined by them.

Little is known about the disciples of Ezra and about the first few generations of the Men of the Great Assembly. Apparently, a number of generations passed between the establishment of the Great Assembly and its demise.

The Great Isaiah Scroll from Qumran Cave I, circa 100 BCE (Israel Museum, Jerusalem)

Shimon HaTzaddik

The next illustrious personage recorded in the Talmud in the chain of the transmission of the Oral Law is Shimon HaTzaddik. He lived at the time of the Second Temple, well over a half century after Ezra and the founding of the Great Assembly. Like Ezra, he was a *kohein*, but unlike Ezra he did serve as a *Kohein Gadol* in the Second Temple. The Talmud records his fateful meeting with Alexander the Great outside the walls of Jerusalem (c. 325 BCE) and the resultant agreement that spared the Temple and the city from destruction by Alexander's army.[9] The Talmud also describes his near prophetic visions and miraculous exploits when he entered the Holy of Holies during the Yom Kippur Temple service.[10] Shimon HaTzaddik also defined the limits of *nazir*—nazirite behavior and vows—and described the difference between asceticism and true holiness.[11]

After the death of Shimon HaTzaddik, his descendants, Shimi and Chonyo, disputed the succession to the office of *Kohein Gadol*. Chonyo eventually immigrated (the Talmud uses the word "fled") to Egypt and established a temple in the district near Alexandria.[12] As we continue to explore the lives of the Talmud's notables in this volume, we unfortunately will find many great

SHIMON HATZADDIK
c. 320 BCE

Teachers
• The Men of the Great Assembly

Colleagues
• The Men of the Great Assembly
• Rabi Dosa ben Hyrkanos

Students
• Antigonus ish Socho

Relatives
• Shimi, son or grandson
• Chonyo, son or grandson

Alexander the Great, Beth Shean, Hellenistic period, 2nd century BCE (Israel Museum, Jerusalem)

THE ORAL LAW OF SINAI

> **"The world stands upon three pillars: Torah, Godly service and human compassion and kindness."**
> *Shimon HaTzaddik - Avos 1*

people whose children, and/or descendants, did not live up to their illustrious pedigree.

The people who filled the role of the *Kohein Gadol* in the Second Temple were many times very questionable, from a religious and spiritual perspective.[13] Shimon HaTzaddik was the exception to this sad story. One of the reasons that he was called "HaTzaddik"—the righteous one—is because out of the more than 300(!) High Priests who served in that position during the time of the Second Temple, he was the sole one who was a completely righteous and holy person.[14]

Ironically, only one statement of his survives in the Talmud.[15] It is an important statement, however, for in it lies the heart of Judaism: He taught that our world stands on Torah, Godly service and human compassion and kindness (Torah, Avodah and Gemilus Chassadim). The purpose, the goal, the parameters of Jewish life and study are defined by these words. As the spiritual successor to Ezra, and the last disciple of the Men of the Great Assembly, he was the father of the Talmud; for with just a few words he illuminates its purpose and focuses its direction: i.e. studying and understanding Torah, Godly service, and exhibiting human kindness and goodness—that is the goal of all study and knowledge of the Oral Law. It is the basis of all of the discussions in the Talmud, all of the give-and-take of *halachah* and logic.

YHD coin (Judah in Hebrew) Jerusalem, 360 BCE (Israel Museum, Jerusalem)

Shimon HaTzaddik wore all of the "crowns" of Judaism. The crowns of the priesthood, of temporal leadership, of Torah greatness and of a good and holy name all rested on his head. He was the person who still had spiritual contact with the generations of *kohanim* and holy men who preceded him from the time of Ezra onward. He was six generations removed from Yehotzadok, the *Kohein Gadol* who returned from the Babylonian exile with Zerubavel. After his death, the *kohanim* could no longer recite the ineffable four-letter name of God in their daily public blessings of the people,[16] for the holy spirit of God's presence was no longer widely felt in Israel.¹⁷ After him, there never would be a single figure who would legitimately wear all of the crowns of Judaism at one time.

In the introduction to his commentary to the Mishnah, Rabbi Moshe ben Maimon (Rambam) lists Rabi Dosa ben Hyrkanos as a colleague of Shimon HaTzaddik.¹⁸ (As opposed to "Rabbi," the title Rabi is pronounced "rah-bee.") Rambam himself realizes the difficulty of this identification, since the Talmud records a conversation between Rabi Dosa and Rabi Akiva, approximately 400 years after Shimon HaTzaddik's time!¹⁹ Rambam therefore states that Rabi Dosa must have lived a very long life! Many writers have questioned the Rambam's theory regarding the time of Rabi Dosa, and therefore place him in the later generation of Raban Yochanan ben Zakkai.²⁰ Without my having the temerity to disagree with Rambam on this matter, I will nevertheless postpone the discussion regarding Rabi Dosa for a later portion of this work.

Obverse side of the coin on opposite page, depicting a lily flower.

After Shimon HaTzaddik and his disciple, Antigonus ish Socho, the period of the *Zugos*—the pairs—commences in the formation of *halachah* and the leadership of the people. From the Talmud itself, it seems that the idea of *Zugos*—pairs of leaders—was an ancient one.²¹ Antigonus was active in the period of time between the beginning of the Greek control of the Land of Israel and the eventual rebellion of the Hasmoneans against that Greek rule. His statement in Avos²² regarding serving God without expecting any reward was misinterpreted by two of his disciples, Tzadok and Baysos, as somehow negating belief in reward and punishment in the World to Come and in the concept of the future revival of the dead. Because of this misinterpretation, and because of the subtle but overwhelming allure of the surrounding Greek culture, they departed from Jewish tradition and created the heretical sects of the *Tzedokim* and *Baysosim*—the Sadducees. Acting upon their new theology, these two apostates gave themselves over to a life of pleasure and luxury, and ate from "dishes of gold and silver all of the days of their lives."²³

Thus, the religious status of the Jewish state was undermined by the Greeks and their culture from both within and without. Around 250 BCE, the rabbis were forced by the Egyptian ruler Ptolemy to translate the written Torah into Greek. They saw this translation as a misfortune,[24] for it introduced not only Greek language into the Jewish society, but it was interpreted by many as an approval of the values of Greek culture itself.

Because of this weakening, it was obvious that the intensification of Torah study, the development of the Oral Law, and increasing the power and influence of Torah scholars would be the only way to mobilize Israel for the struggles that faced it. It would be the *Zugos* who would undertake that struggle to develop the framework of Torah life that would triumph over the Greeks, the Jewish Hellenists and the Sadducees.

Jerusalem from the Road Leading to Bethany by David Roberts, R.A., England, 1796-1864, published in 1842 (Library of Congress)

The Zugos

From approximately 180 BCE to 30 BCE five sets of *Zugos* spiritually led the Jewish people. One of the pair would be the *Nasi*—the "leader"—while the other would serve as the *Av Beis Din*—the head of the court system and of the yeshivah.[25] The era of the *Zugos* was one of the most turbulent periods in Second Temple times. Within this century and a half, numerous momentous events took place: Chanukah; the rise of the Hasmoneans to power; the civil war between the Sadducees and the rabbis known as the *Perushim*; the rise of Roman power in the Middle East; the conquest of Jerusalem by Pompey; and the destruction of the Hasmonean dynasty by Herod.

But the development of the Oral Law and the study of Torah nevertheless gained momentum despite this maelstrom of political uncertainty and constant national upheaval. One must view with awe the ability of the rabbis and Torah scholars to concentrate on the preservation and development of Torah, especially of the Oral Law, under such trying circumstances.

The tradition of the Oral Law from the time of Moses till the end of the period of the *Knesses HaGedolah* had been kept and updated privately throughout the ages in what were called *"megillos sesarim"*—the "hidden megillos." During this period, they were now made more public and expanded, eventually becoming *"Mishnah Rishona"*—the first text of Mishnah.[26]

THE ZUGOS
c. 210 BCE – c. 10 BCE

Yosi ben Yoezer and Yosi ben Yochanan

YOSI BEN YOEZER AND YOSI BEN YOCHANAN
c. 210 BCE

Teacher
• Antigonus ish Socho

Colleagues
• Matisyahu and the original Hasmoneans

Students
• Yehoshua ben Prachyah
• Nitai HaArbeli

"May your house be a meeting place for the scholars."
Yosi ben Yoezer

Yosi (Yosef) ben Yoezer, the *Nasi*, and Yosi (Yosef) ben Yochanan, the *Av Beis Din*, who formed the first pair of the *Zugos*, were the disciples of Antigonus ish Socho. They viewed with horror the apostasy of their former fellow colleagues, Tzadok and Baysos. The twin evils of denial of Torah and the Oral Law with its attendant principle of reward and punishment, and of living a hedonistic Greek lifestyle, which the apostasy of Tzadok and Baysos represented, was countered by the two Yosis. They issued a ruling that anyone who left the Land of Israel became ritually impure and that glass (crystal) vessels could become ritually impure.[27] Glass was extremely expensive and hard to come by in those times, and it served as the symbol of wealth and luxurious living. The issue of ritual impurity was taken very seriously by the Jewish populace of the Land of Israel at that time. It vitally affected one's ability to participate in any form of Temple worship and had many other implications in daily life. The goal of these decrees was to inhibit assimilation into Greek society by traveling to Greece and becoming enmeshed in a pagan, God-denying culture that negated the Jewish value of reward and punishment and promoted a hedonistic pursuit of luxuries.

The era of these first of the *Zugos* was an especially difficult one for the Jews, for it was then that the coercion and persecution of

Jews and Judaism by Antiochus Epiphanus began and took force. The influence of the times can be seen in the family tragedies that befell Yosi ben Yoezer himself. He had a son who did not behave in a proper Jewish manner.[28] Moreover, sentenced to death for flaunting Greek orders against teaching Torah publicly, he was led to his execution by his own nephew, who taunted him about the apparent unwillingness of God to save him from terrible torture and death.[29] But Yosi ben Yoezer responded to his nephew's taunts with such expressions of faith and devotion to Judaism that the nephew himself repented and gained eternal life.[30]

(The phenomenon of close relatives leading their own loved ones to death or exile in the name of foreign cultures or causes has often been repeated in Jewish history. During the era of Communist tyranny in Eastern Europe in the twentieth century, many great rabbis and *Chasidic* leaders were betrayed and doomed by their very own flesh and blood, all in the name of the new utopian culture that would save humankind.)

Until the time of Yosi ben Yoezer and Yosi ben Yochanan there are no recorded disputes between the scholars as to *halachah* and practical behavior in Jewish life. As mentioned above, all such matters were decided by the Sanhedrin and the great scholars of Israel, and their word was final. Thus, there were no lasting disputes about Jewish law. The fact that there was only one head of the Jewish establishment—such as Ezra or Shimon HaTzaddik—and that the scholars were free of persecution by outside forces, also minimized the chance for lasting disputes in *halachah*.

But with the shared authority of the *Zugos*, and the persecution of the Greeks, coupled with the rise of societal fragmentation occa-

Glass Plate, Cave of letters, 2nd century CE (Israel Museum, Jerusalem)

sioned by the rise of the heretical sects of *Tzedokim* and *Baysosim*, the days of a single decision in halachic matters waned. The first recorded halachic dispute was between Yosi ben Yoezer and Yosi ben Yochanan regarding the permissibility of placing of one's hands on the head of an animal that was to be sacrificed in the Temple on a holiday.[31] Placing one's hands on the animal was a mandated part of the service of bringing a sacrificial offering in the Temple. The halachic question concerned the concept of "work" with animals on the holiday. By pressing one's hands on the animal, thus essentially supporting oneself on the animal, a serious issue of "work" with the animal occurred. Until this issue was raised, there were no previous halachic matters left unresolved or in dispute.

This halachic dispute continued for the entire period of the *Zugos* without resolution. Hillel and Shammai, almost two centuries after Yosi ben Yoezer and Yosi ben Yochanan, still disputed the very same issue. It is interesting to note that during the entire time of the *Zugos*, when this dispute still was present, it was always the *Nasi* who forbade the placing of the hands on the animal and the *Av Beis Din* who permitted it, until the time of Hillel and Shammai, when these roles were reversed. It is clear that the method of disputation on halachic matters began with Yosi ben Yoezer and Yosi ben Yochanan. But they had only one matter in dispute. Their spiritual heirs in following generations of the development of the Talmud would debate and dispute hundreds of such issues.

In a cryptic mishnah that appears in *Eduyos*, chapter 8, mishnah 4, Yosi ben Yoezer is called "Yosi the lenient." This is because he permitted three matters that the earlier custom—though not the *halachah*—had apparently forbidden. In the Talmud, any individual or rabbinic court that explicitly permits three matters that previously were held to be forbidden is automatically called "lenient." Yosi ben Yoezer and Yosi ben Yochanan are described as "*Eshkolos—shehakol bo*"—people who possessed "everything," i.e. extraordinarily talented, multifaceted individuals and great scholars. All of Torah and morality, intellect and vision, was combined within them. They proved to be the last individuals granted that title in the times of the Mishnah.[32]

> "May your house be open wide to all and may the poor become part of your household."
> *Yosi ben Yochanan*

Yehoshua ben Prachyah and Nitai HaArbeli

The second pair of the *Zugos* was composed of Yehoshua ben Prachyah and Nitai HaArbeli. They rose to power after the Chanukah victory of the Hasmoneans (165-161 BCE) and their main activity was during the reign of Yochanan Hyrkanos, the grandson of Mattisyahu, the founder of the Hasmonean dynasty and the son of Shimon, the first of the Hasmonean kings. They seemed to have served in office for more than half a century, since we find Yehoshua ben Prachyah still active in the turbulent times of Alexander Yanai's reign as king of Israel. Yochanan, and then Yanai, both conducted wars against the *Perushim*, the scholars of Israel. During that time, Yehoshua ben Prachyah escaped to Alexandria.[33] When Yanai relented and his overt persecution of the *Perushim* ended, Yehoshua ben Prachyah returned from Egypt to resume his role as *Nasi* with Nitai HaArbeli remaining as *Av Beis Din*.

Yehoshua is the author of the famous statement of attitude towards public office: "Originally, anyone who proposed to me that I should become *Nasi*—I wished to feed him to the lions. However, after I became the *Nasi*, if anyone would propose to me that I relinquish that office, I would douse him with boiling water!"[34]

No halachic opinions, except for the matter of placing the hands on the animal for the holiday sacrifice, are offered in the Talmud in

YEHOSHUA BEN PRACHYAH AND NITAI HAARBEILI
c. 165 BCE

Teachers
- Yosi ben Yoezer
- Yosi ben Yochanan

Colleagues
- Yochanan Hyrkanos, the Hasmonean king

Students
- Yehudah ben Tabai
- Shimon ben Shatach

"Judge every human being in a favorable manner."
Yehoshua ben Prachyah

"Never despair because of evil happenings [in the world]"
Nitai HaArbeli

the name of Nitai HaArbeli. Yehoshua ben Prachyah also receives sparing mention in the Talmud.³⁵ An opinion of his regarding the ritual purity of wheat that arrives from Alexandria,³⁶ an opinion that was contested by the majority of scholars, appears to be the only other halachic comment of his in Talmudic literature. The statements on ethics and morals of this pair of the *Zugos* appear in Avos,³⁷ as do similar statements of all of the other *Zugos* as well.

Yehoshua and Nitai operated within the confines of a Sanhedrin whose members were appointed by the Hasmonean kings and consisted mainly of *Tzedokim*/Sadducees. Hence, the influence and teachings of Yehoshua and Nitai were deemed by the Hasmonean government and its court as not binding, but were nevertheless considered valid by large sections of the Jewish society who remained loyal to tradition and to the teachings of the Oral Law.

Jerusalem from the Mount of Olives by David Roberts, R.A., England, 1796-1864, published in 1842 (Library of Congress)

Yehudah ben Tabai and Shimon ben Shatach

The third set of *Zugos* was by far the most controversial of these leaders of Israel. Yehudah ben Tabai and Shimon ben Shatach served during the reign of the volatile and violent Hasmonean king, Alexander Yanai, and after his death, during the regency of his pious queen, Shlomzion (Salome Alexandra). A brother of Shlomzion, Shimon ben Shatach became the most dominant figure in Jewish life during her reign. There was a difference of opinion among the later rabbis of the Mishnah as to which of the two—Shimon ben Shatach or Yehudah ben Tabai—was the *Nasi* and which one was the *Av Beis Din*.[38] Both were exiled to Egypt in the time of the persecution of the *Perushim* by Alexander Yanai. Shimon ben Shatach returned to the Land of Israel during the latter days of Alexander Yanai and reconciled with his brother-in-law, and again became a member of the Sanhedrin, eventually becoming the *Nasi* during that time.

The original dispute between Shimon and the king was personal, stemming from their agreement to free 300 destitute nazirites from their vows. Both Alexander Yanai and Shimon ben Shatach undertook to each free 150 of the nazirites. The king freed 150 of the nazirites by giving them money to pay for the necessary sacrificial offerings in the Temple that would then acquit them from their nazarite vows, while Shimon freed his 150 nazirites with a

YEHUDAH BEN TABAI AND SHIMON BEN SHATACH
c. 130 BCE

Teachers
- Yehoshua ben Prachyah
- Nitai HaArbeli

Colleagues
- Choni HaMaagel
- Todos ish Romi
- Alexander Yanai, the Hasmonean king
- Shlomzion HaMalka, the Hasmonean queen

Students
- Shmaya
- Avtalyon

Relatives
- Shlomzion HaMalka was the sister of Shimon ben Shatach
- Alexander Yanai was Shimon ben Shatach's brother-in-law

halachic retraction of their vows by a rabbinic court. Alexander Yanai felt that he was cheated and was enraged at Shimon.[39] There were other personal incidents in their relationship that further aggravated their dislike of each other.[40]

However, their main dispute concerned the king's persecution of the *Perushim* due to their objection to his serving as both king and High Priest simultaneously.[41] The king now favored the *Tzedokim*, and under his rule the Sanhedrin continued to be dominated by them. However, at the end of his life, Alexander realized his error and, as mentioned above, reconciled with Shimon and with the *Perushim*. Shimon purged the Sanhedrin of its *Tzedokim* members and headed a Sanhedrin of properly worthy Torah scholars.[42] After the death of the king, he sent for Yehudah ben Tabai to return to Israel and serve as *Nasi*.[43] It is not clear whether Yehudah actually returned and assumed that role.

Yehudah ben Tabai and Shimon ben Shatach disagreed as to whether the *halachah* allowed certain apparently extralegal matters to be employed regarding the punishment of a false witness in order to "remove [their false interpretation of the written Torah] from the hearts of the *Tzedokim*."[44] The *Tzedokim*, because of their refusal to recognize the Oral Law as binding, employed different rules than the Oral Law mandated regarding the definition and punishment of false witnesses. Because of this disagreement and its tragic consequence—that a man was wrongfully put to death by a rabbinic court—Yehudah ben Tabai accepted upon himself not to decide any other matters of *halachah* without obtaining the prior opinion and approval of Shimon ben Shatach. He also regularly visited the grave of the false witness who was wrongfully executed and begged his forgiveness. Except for the dispute regarding the placing of the hands on the animal for the holiday sacrifice and the dispute regarding the punishment of a false witness mentioned above, there are no other halachic decisions in the Talmud rendered in the name of Yehudah ben Tabai. As is the case of all of the *Zugos*, there are moral statements of his recorded in Avos.[45]

Yet it is obvious from the Talmud itself that Shimon ben Shatach was the most dominant figure of his age. As mentioned above, most

> **"When litigants accept upon themselves the judgment of the court and abide by it, both parties [to the litigation] are to be seen as worthy and correct."**
>
> *Yehudah ben Tabai*

of his public activity was during the nine-year reign of his sister, Queen Shlomzion. His accomplishments during that time are impressive. He established a school system for the country.[46] In matters of the *kesubah* (marital contract), he strengthened the rights of the wife so as to prevent the husband from quickly and unjustly divorcing her.[47] He attempted to discipline Todos Ish Romi for allowing roasted goat meat to be used at the Pesach Seder in Rome, a violation, Shimon felt, of the edict not to eat *Kodashim b'chutz*—meat of Temple sacrifices outside of the Temple or Jerusalem.[48] He also disapproved of the public miracle of Choni HaMaagel which ended a long drought in the Land of Israel, but ruefully admitted that he was powerless to do anything about it since "the Lord does your [Choni's] will!"[49]

"Be careful with your words."
Shimon ben Shatach

It was during the time of Shimon ben Shatach that great prosperity returned to the Land of Israel. The Talmud attributes this improvement to the pious influence of Shimon ben Shatach in raising the moral standards, Torah knowledge and religious observance of the general populace.[50]

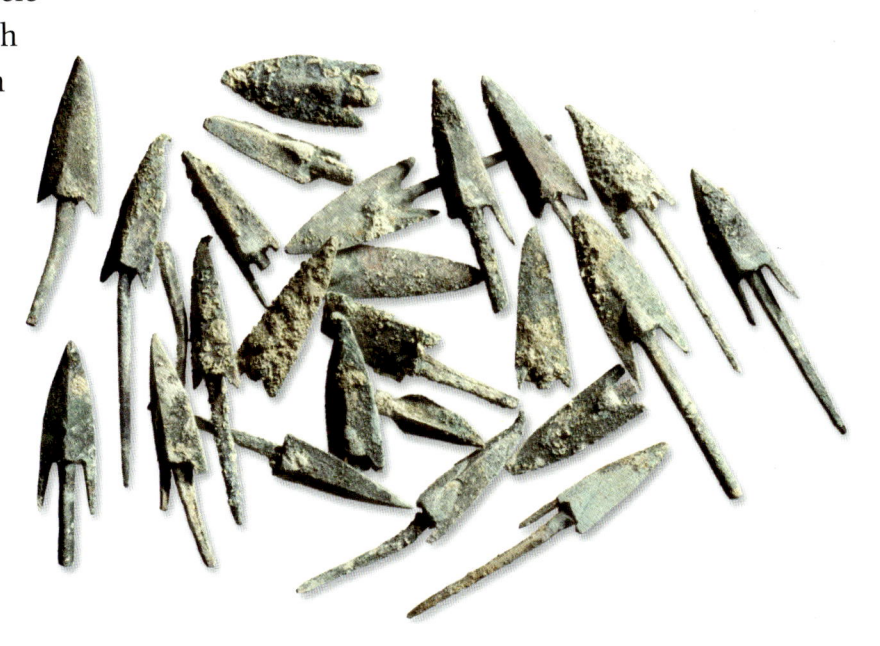

Arrowheads found in the citadel of Jerusalem, dating from Hasmonean revolt

Shimon himself was of impeccable character and saintly behavior. He once purchased a donkey from an Arab and found a precious stone in the donkey's neck strap. He returned the gem to the seller, stating, "I purchased a donkey, not a precious stone." The Arab exclaimed: "Blessed be the God of Shimon ben Shatach!"[51] The Arab was sensitive enough to perceive that it was not Shimon ben Shatach's personal honesty alone that returned the item to him. Rather, it was the discipline of God's moral law—which is always the hallmark of the great men and women of Israel—that stood behind Shimon ben Shatach's act of honesty. Through Shimon ben Shatach, all human beings were able to glimpse the God of Israel.

There was tragedy in his life too. The pagan practice and belief in witchcraft was rampant in the Jewish society of his time, and Shimon ben Shatach attempted to eradicate it. As witchcraft was a strong moneymaking industry, its supporters took revenge against Shimon by falsely accusing his son of a capital crime. On the basis of false witnesses, who were hired by Shimon's enemies, the son was convicted and sentenced to death. Even though the witnesses later recanted, Shimon's son was nevertheless executed.[52]

Despite a very turbulent life in a society of constant governmental and judicial violence, his memory is enshrined in the Talmud and in the collective memory of Israel as a hero, a *tzaddik* and a great leader. Shimon died in 68 BCE and his sister, Queen Shlomzion, died two years later.

Alexander Yanai had brought the Jewish commonwealth to military power and expanded its borders, while Queen Shlomzion and Shimon ben Shatach had raised the nation to spiritual and educational excellence and to economic prosperity. All of these achievements were about to be squandered by a bitter civil war between Alexander's two sons, Yehudah Hyrkan and Aristoblus. Yehudah was a person of soft temperament and a deeply religious person who was attached to the *Perushim*. Aristoblus, who assumed the role of High Priest even during his mother's lifetime, was a schemer and determined to wrest all power for himself.

A bitter war between the brothers broke out for control of the government. Aristoblus allied himself with the *Tzedokim* and besieged Jericho, the stronghold of his brother, eventually gaining total power. Yehudah Hyrkan was defeated and temporarily retired from public life. However, influenced by the malevolent Antipater (a general and governor of a Judean province during the reign of Alexander Yanai) Yehudah Hyrkan renewed the war against his brother, besieging him in Jerusalem and eventually in the Temple Mount compound.

Both sides were guilty of terrible atrocities and desecrations. Swine were sent up the walls of the Temple instead of the usual kosher sacrificial animals.[53] Both sides attempted to draw the Romans into the conflict and it was Pompey who eventually decided the matter in favor of the pliable Yehudah Hyrkan. It was akin to inviting the lion into the house to get rid of the pesky cat. How does one get the lion out afterwards?

The Hasmoneans were never able to oust Rome, and it was Rome's perfidious agent, Antipater, who now actually ruled the country. Pompey had conducted a fearful massacre of Jews in Jerusalem in order to impose Roman rule, but he spared the Temple and allowed nominal Jewish government to continue under the weak king, Yehudah Hyrkan. By 63 BCE, all of the accomplishments of the Hasmoneans were undone. Judea had become a vassal state to Rome.

Coins of Alexander Yanai, a king of the Hasmonean dynasty

Shmaya and Avtalyon

SHMAYA AND AVTALYON
c. 80 BCE
Time of Antipater and Herod

Teachers
Yehudah ben Tabai
Shimon ben Shatach

Colleagues
Bnei Bseira

Students
Hillel
Shammai

In this period of the disintegration of Jewish temporal power, the chain of Torah tradition was carried forward by Shmaya and Avtalyon. These two disciples of Yehudah ben Tabai and Shimon ben Shatach[54] were converts to Judaism[55] or descended from families of converts.[56] The Talmud teaches us that they were descended from Sennacherib, the Assyrian king who exiled the Ten Tribes of Israel and besieged Jerusalem during the First Temple reign of King Chizkiyah of Judah.[57] Shmaya and Avtalyon were revered by the common people as well as their colleagues.[58]

Unlike their teacher, Shimon ben Shatach, Shmaya and Avtalyon withdrew from public life and governmental issues. They concentrated almost exclusively on building the inner empire of Israel—the Torah, its *halachah* and moral values—the creation of an eternal structure that would see Israel through all of the storms of the future.

Shmaya had originally attempted to hold back the destructive force of Antipater and his sons, especially of the megalomaniac murderer, Herod. As head of the Sanhedrin, he brought Herod to trial before that body for the murder of a certain Chizkiyah and his supporters in the struggle for control of the Galilee. Herod was then the Roman appointee over the Galilee and had already acquired his deserved murderous reputation. Thus, when Herod appeared before the Sanhedrin fully armed and with his equally armed bodyguards, the other members of the Sanhedrin refused to prosecute him. Shmaya warned them: "Know that the man whom you now wish to free from his murderous liability will eventually repay you by killing all of you!"[59] Shmaya's dire prediction was fulfilled in bitter completeness.

It seems that after this disappointing and dangerous experience, Shmaya realized that the hope of Jewish survival now lay purely in the spiritual development and not in confrontation with the authorities of the government. He felt that open opposition to the evil government would be futile and that it would eventually fall from the weight of its own sins.

Shmaya was a fervent advocate of the importance of productive labor and commercial enterprise.[60] As with the other *Zugos*, Shmaya and Avtalyon were in dispute over the matter of placing the hands on the animal for the holiday sacrifice.[61] There are very few other matters of *halachah* that are directly quoted in their names. There are many references to them however, regarding halachic matters in statements made by their disciples, and even in later generations.[62] In a time of terrible turmoil and of mounting terror and violence, Shmaya and Avtalyon constructed this inner firewall of Torah and tradition within Jewish life. The Mishnah and the Talmud would later be based on their efforts and would thus be protected from the external vicissitudes of national destruction and exile. But perhaps their most significant accomplishment was in bringing to Torah prominence and eternal Jewish leadership their extraordinary disciple, Hillel.

> "Because you members of the Sanhedrin refuse to take action against Herod out of fear, know you that he will kill you anyway."
> *Shmaya*

Coin issued by Mattathias Antigonus

> "Wise men, be careful with your public statements lest you be forced to flee into exile."
> *Avtalyon*

Hillel and Shammai

HILLEL AND SHAMMAI
c. 30 BCE

Teachers
• Shmaya
• Avtalyon

Colleagues
• Menachem
• Bnei Bseira

Students
• Rabi Yochanan ben Zakai
• Yonasan ben Uziel
• Rabi Tzadok min HaKohanim
• Bava ben Buta
• Dustai ish Kfar Yavneh
• Yoezer ish HaBirah

Relatives
• Son of Hillel: Raban Shimon ben Hillel

The last pair of the *Zugos* was Hillel and Shammai. To a great extent, if such judgments can be made at all, Hillel and Shammai left the most lasting imprint of all of the *Zugos* on the future generations of Torah scholarship and on the development of the Talmud. Hillel is the more famous of the two. The Talmud suggests that if Ezra was Moshe, so to speak, then Hillel was Ezra:[63]

When the Torah was forgotten from Israel, Ezra arose from Bavel and reestablished it. When it was again forgotten [because of the persecution of the *Perushim* and the political and military turmoil in the Land of Israel] *Hillel the Bavli arose and again reestablished it.*[64]

Born in Bavel/Babylonia to a distinguished family of scholars (and through his mother a descendant of King David),[65] Hillel immigrated to the Land of Israel to study Torah from Shmaya and Avtalyon. Poor in money, but enormously rich in spirit and ambition, Hillel earned his meager livelihood as a woodchopper.[66] He risked his health—and even his life—to study Torah: Once, during the winter, when he could not afford to pay the daily fee for attending the lectures of Shmaya and Avtalyon, Hillel climbed onto the roof of the building and listened to the lecture through the skylight of the building. He nearly froze to death. After he was found, he was permitted to attend the lectures free of charge and he eventually became the premier student of Shmaya and Avtalyon.[67] After Hillel, poverty could no longer be used as an excuse for not studying Torah,⁶⁸ for he had achieved distinction despite his financial circumstances.

Hillel returned to Bavel for an unknown period of time and returned to the Land of Israel only after the deaths of Shmaya and Avtalyon. Apparently, his return to Judea coincided with the beginning of Herod's rule over the country in approximately 30 BCE. Hillel was now supported financially by his brother, Shavna, in a classic Zevulun/Yissachar arrangement.⁶⁹ (The Torah scholar agrees to share his reward in the World to Come for his Torah achievements with the person who supports him financially in this world.) Hillel's scholarship in all areas of Torah (and other knowledge as well) was now known and highly respected throughout the Jewish world.⁷⁰ But as of yet, he held no public office or official position in Jewish society.

Confusion reigned in the ranks of the Sanhedrin after the deaths of Shmaya and Avtalyon due to the rise to power of Antipater and later of his sons, especially Herod. Apparently, instead of one *Nasi*, an entire family—the Bnei Bseira—assumed that office collectively. The *Av Beis Din* was a person named Menachem. By then, the Sanhedrin had lost much of its independence, influence and power.⁷¹

Menachem left the position of *Av Beis Din* during the reign of Antipater,⁷² and there is some dispute about what happened to him afterward. The Talmud offers a few opinions: One is that he went into the service of the government, and another opinion is that he "went out to lead a bad way of life and culture *[l'tarbus raah]*"⁷³ This second opinion in the Talmud is most probably a reference to his then joining either the *Tzedokim*/Sadducees or the *Eeseeyim*/Essenes. This latter group was a sect that emphasized spiritual and bodily purity over all else in Judaism. They lived in desert caves, remained celibate, spent their time in meditation and isolation and studied mysterious works. It was from this group that the early sect of Christians arose.

In any event, Menachem was replaced as *Av Beis Din* by Shammai.⁷⁴ The Talmud⁷⁵ also tells us that Menachem went to work for the Herodian royal house. He took with him 80 pairs of students wearing royal raiment.⁷⁶ They forsook the study hall of Torah for

> "Love peace, pursue peace, love one's fellow humans and bring them closer to Torah."
> *Hillel*

the supposed riches of governmental power and largesse. No wonder the Talmud has no more to say about Menachem and his students.

A short time thereafter, Hillel returned to the Land of Israel, as noted above. In the famous discussion with the Bnei Bseira about the proper procedure to follow regarding the paschal lamb sacrifice when the time of the sacrifice itself falls on a Shabbos, the Bnei Bseira resigned their office in favor of Hillel.[77] Thus both Hillel and Shammai rose to their positions of leadership through the resignations of their predecessors in those positions. It seems obvious that Heaven decided that Hillel and Shammai would be the only right people to guide Israel during that most turbulent and depressing of times. And they proved themselves more than equal to the task.

For the first time, Hillel established in writing the *midos*—the individual tools of methodology by which the Oral Law could be derived from the written Torah itself. His list of those *midos* was seven in number.[78] These seven *midos* had been the basis for the study and expansion of the Oral Law throughout all of the previous generations. However, Hillel was the one who codified them and revealed their methods of elucidation of the Torah to the wider public. Hillel's seven *midos* became the basis for the final list of the thirteen *midos* of the Oral Law formulated by Rabbi Yishmael over a century after Hillel's death. The use of these *midos* required great Torah knowledge and exacting logic and analysis in order to prove effective. Some of them also required tradition from previous generations, even back to Moses and Sinai, in order to be employed. A great deal of the Talmud is occupied with the use of these *midos* and with differing opinions among the rabbinic scholars as to whether the logic of the particular issue involved justifies conclusions proposed by their use. Hillel and his colleague Shammai, therefore, are the initiators of the great give-and-take debate that characterizes the Talmud and the corpus of all Jewish law since their time.

Hillel and Shammai themselves disagreed regarding only three matters of *halachah* and practical Jewish law.[79] Up to their time, with the exception of the ongoing debate regarding the placing of one's hands on a holiday sacrifice—a debate that had not been re-

> "Say little and do much."
> *Shammai*

solved in spite of over five generations of discussion[80]—all halachic questions had been successfully resolved, so that there was a unanimity of decision and practice in Israel. The disagreements between Hillel and Shammai were therefore viewed as being a negative factor in Jewish life.[81]

Both Hillel and Shammai saw in the spiritual development of the Jewish people the key to the survival of Israel under the murderous and tyrannical rule of Herod and his Roman masters. The oppression of the rabbis and the scholars by Herod no longer allowed for their convening openly to decide matters of *halachah* and policy. As Hillel and Shammai each had established a yeshivah, there developed two major schools of Torah learning and Oral Law development—the House of Hillel and the House of Shammai. The schools reflected the opinions, worldview and temperaments of their founders. The House of Hillel was larger in numbers than the House of Shammai. This was a direct result of Hillel's attitude towards teaching Torah to all Jews, no matter their background and pedigree, while Shammai stated that Torah should be taught only to "wise, humble, financially independent people of high family pedigree"[82] for he wholeheartedly felt that the peace of mind and intense concentration needed for successful Torah study would be most difficult to achieve if the student is poverty-stricken or of below average intellect. The former group was understandably much more numerous than was the latter one.

Cave where Hillel HaZaken is buried, Mount Meron

Hillel and Shammai also disagreed on the attitude towards potential converts to Judaism. During the centuries of the development of the Mishnah (c. 200 BCE to 200 CE), there was a wave of conversions to Judaism. The Hasmonean kings followed a policy of mass conversions of conquered tribes and neighbors. This coercive and overly permissive policy brought about sad results individually and nationally, of which Antipater and his family may serve as a prime example. Nevertheless, the true and righteous converts to Judaism brought remarkable talent, devotion and exemplary leadership into the ranks of Jewish society. As noted earlier, Shmaya and Avtalyon (there is a difference of opinion as to whether they themselves were converts or the children of converts) were examples of this enormous contribution to Jewish vitality and strength. Hillel, who always emphasized that his greatness and knowledge of Torah was primarily a product of having studied at the feet of Shmaya and Avtalyon,[83] apparently was willing to accept converts whom he felt would eventually come to fulfill fully the requirements of Jewish ritual and moral behavior.[84] Shammai took a much more cautious attitude towards converts and conversions to Judaism.[85]

Tomb of Shammai, Mount Meron

Hillel appears in the Talmud as a pliant, humble, tolerant person.[86] He has enormous patience and is slow to anger or frustration.[87] His motto in life and in Torah is "Do not do unto others what is hateful unto you."[88] He is optimistic to a fault[89] and supremely confident in Divine judgment and retribution to evildoers.[90] He mocks the pursuit of material luxuries in this world and exalts the never-ending struggle to achieve peace, wisdom and a meaningful life.[91] He cautions against short-tempered teachers, people of boorish behavior, being over engaged in business and work, and admonishes students who are too afraid or embarrassed to speak their minds and express their doubts.[92] Hillel also demanded that no one should sever himself from the general Jewish community; should never be overconfident in one's piety and abilities; and to always attempt to put one's self in the other person's position before hastening to judgment or comment.[93]

Hillel had unquestioning faith in God's goodness and in His ability to provide under all circumstances.[94] He trusted and believed in the innate wisdom and goodness of the people of Israel. Even in matters of *halachah*, Hillel trusted the behavior of the Jewish masses. "If they [the people of Israel currently] are not prophets, they are still the children of prophets."[95]

Hillel lived a very long life[96] and in his sterling character traits and wise teachings he remains forever as the paragon of virtue, Torah instruction and holiness in Jewish life.[97] Worthy of the Divine spirit resting upon him,[98] the eulogy for him was simple: "That great pious man; that great man of humility; the true disciple of Ezra!"[99]

Hillel's colleague, Shammai, had a far different personality. The Talmud refers to him as being a *kapdan*[100]—a person who was meticulous, strict with himself and others, and given to impatience with human folly. He was cautious and conservative by nature, always providing for tomorrow with the resources of today.[101] It was not that Shammai had less faith than Hillel in God's ability to provide for tomorrow: it was rather his sense of meticulous inner discipline that forced him to do whatever he could so that the sacred and most important morrow—the Shabbos and Yom Tov—would

> **"Do not do unto others what is hateful unto you."**
> *Hillel*

be well provided for in advance. When his grandson was yet a newborn infant, Shammai brought him into the protective and holy shade of the succah on the festival of *Succos*.[102] It was never too early for Shammai to prepare himself and others for the observance of mitzvos and Torah study. Little is known about Shammai's personal life, and few of his sayings and teachings, relative to those of Hillel, are mentioned in the Talmud.

As mentioned earlier, the Talmud tells us that Shammai was made the head of the court after Menachem retired from the post.[103] Due to Shammai's restrictive policy of admitting only gifted, wealthy and pious students to his yeshiva, the students of Shammai were considered by the Talmud to be on the whole "*mechadedei tfei*"—sharper, quicker, and more intellectually brilliant than those of Hillel.[104] The students of Shammai were willing to give up their lives to uphold some laws and teachings of their master.[105]

In most instances in the Talmud, the halachic decision favored the opinion of Hillel's disciples, since they were the majority in numbers;[106] a *bas kol*—heavenly revelation—sided with them; and because of their humility in always quoting the opinion of Shammai's disciples along with their own (and in most instances, quoting that opinion before advancing their own).[107] Nevertheless, the opinions of Shammai and his disciples are also followed in a number of instances in the Talmud.[108] There were times that Hillel himself sat humbly at the feet of Shammai and accepted his opinion.[109]

Shammai and Hillel march together throughout the Talmud and through all of the ages of Jewish history. In Jewish hearts and minds, as well as on the pages of the Talmud itself, they are inseparable. The heavenly proclamation that "They are both the words of the living God!"[110] became the motto of Israel regarding its relationship to Hillel and Shammai and to their respective schools and disciples.

With Hillel and Shammai, the development of the Mishnah took on a new phase. Because of the fact that under Hillel's influence the numbers of students studying Torah was greatly expanded, there were students who were not yet qualified to decide halachic issues who nevertheless took part in the debates between

> **"They are both the words of the living God!"**
> *Talmud*

the schools of Hillel and Shammai. Because of this, the original number of disputes between Hillel and Shammai, which were only three or four in number, grew to over 300 and there was a danger that there would be two Torahs in Israel.[111] Each of the schools also kept journals and notes of their halachic opinions and teachings. These were early forms of the Mishnah that were now added to the previous journals of the First Mishnah that had existed for centuries. But since the journals of the disciples of Shammai were materially different from those of the students of Hillel, the danger of "two Torahs" was real and imminent.[112] Therefore, the rabbis decided and proclaimed that the Mishnah of the school of Shammai was of no authority relative to the Mishnah of the school of Hillel.[113] As mentioned above, the Mishnah of the school of Hillel always included within it the opinions of the school of Shammai as well, and therefore was a complete record of halachic debate and opinion up to its time.[114] It would be this privately studied journal of the school of Hillel that would form the basis for all later development of the Mishnah and the Talmud.[115]

It was also from this point onwards, due to the persecution of the *Perushim* by Herod and later by the Romans directly, that it became more and more difficult to settle halachic questions by consensus or vote. The ability of the rabbis to convene was severely constrained, and thus opposing opinions were not easily debatable or reconcilable. For the 50 years preceding the destruction of the Temple in 70 CE, the chaos in Jewish life in the Land of Israel was insufferable, and the rabbis found it very difficult to establish any central spiritual authority.

Hillel's successors as the *Nasi*[116] fought valiantly to keep the ship of Torah afloat in the sea of violence, paganism and persecution that raged around them. It was perhaps the bitterness of those times that forced the students of Hillel to rethink their position and agree with the school of Shammai—that humankind would have been better off if it had never been created. But they added that now—since we were already created—one should always carefully examine one's deeds in order to improve one's personal behavior and that of human behavior generally.[117]

THE ORAL LAW OF SINAI

Page from the 15th-century Darmstadt Haggadah written by Israel ben Meir of Heidelberg, the lower section depicting the sages and four sons "reclining" and discussing the exodus from Egypt (The Darmstadt University Library)

Hillel also produced many *takanos*—rabbinic ordinances advanced to answer pressing social and economic problems of his society.[118] The entire period of the Mishnah would see many such *takanos* created by the leaders of the Torah institutions and the Sanhedrin. Not all of the *takanos* proposed by the rabbis would be accepted by the masses of Israel. The public, so to speak, had a right of veto over new decrees and ordinances.[119]

Hillel's *takanos* were easily accepted by Israel, and this certainly was due, in part, to his holy personality. The people sensed that he would never abuse his power or encourage radical programs and impractical rules of behavior. They sensed that he had the public's welfare at heart and not his own benefit or power.[120] His personal customs and halachic behavior were preserved in addition to his *takanos*. A prime example of this is *Koreich*—the *matzoh/maror* "sandwich" that is an integral part of the Pesach Seder service[121] about which the *Haggadah* says, "Thus did Hillel."

But most importantly, his work and his influence were preserved throughout the ages by the Jewish people who loved him as he loved them. Generations later, the highest compliment that could be paid to a Jewish spiritual leader was that "he was a disciple of Hillel."[122]

Shammai's disciples who are known to us are only four in number. They were Rabi Tzadok min HaKohanim, Bava ben Buta, Dustai ish Kfar Yavneh and Yoezer ish Habirah. Interestingly enough, all four are known to us because of their modesty, goodness to others (even enemies), piety and moderation.[123] Any presumed image of a rigid Shammai must therefore be tempered by observing the attitudes and behavior of his closest disciples.

It would be no exaggeration to say that Hillel and Shammai—joined together as they are in Jewish history and scholarship—fathered the Talmud. It was their spirit and methods of debate, erudition and pedagogy that dominated the Jewish world for the next centuries when this monumental work was created, edited and published.

SECTION II

RABAN SHIMON BEN HILLEL TO RABI AKIVA

C. 30 BCE - 200 CE

*Map of the Jewish Land
Under the Romans,
Willem Albert Bachiene,
Dutch, 1712-1753 (Israel
Museum, Jerusalem)*

Transmitting Tradition

After the deaths of Hillel and Shammai, their two great schools of Torah study, with their numerous disciples, held sway. For nearly the next two centuries, the schools of Shammai and Hillel would produce almost all of the Torah scholars of Israel. It was they who brought the Mishnah to its final form in the time of Rabi Yehudah HaNasi, a descendant of Hillel himself.

Hillel's immediate successor as the *Nasi* and the spiritual leader of Israel was his son, Shimon. He, in turn, was succeeded by his own son, Gamliel, known as Raban Gamliel HaZaken (The Elder). I take the liberty of identifying him here as Raban Gamliel I. He was in turn succeeded by his son, Raban Shimon ben Gamliel. Again, since this name was used by a number of different great scholars, I will refer to him as Raban Shimon ben Gamliel I. These four scholars—Hillel, Shimon, Gamliel I and Shimon ben Gamliel I—occupied the office of the *Nasi* for the last 100 years of the Second Temple's existence.[1] During this terrible time of upheaval, rebellion, civil war, criminal gangs and Christian beginnings, these sages somehow managed to keep the Jewish people going and succeeded in stabilizing in part the daily Jewish religious and temporal existence.

Raban Shimon ben Hillel

RABAN SHIMON BEN HILLEL
c. 10 BCE

Teacher
• Hillel

Colleague
• Yonasan ben Uziel

Students
• Raban Gamliel I
• Shmuel HaKatan

Relatives
• Father: Hillel
• Son: Raban Gamliel I

"He was the mufla sheb'sanhedrin — the exceptional chosen leader, the greatest scholar and decisor of the Sanhedrin."

HaTalmud V'Yotzrav

Very little is known about Hillel's son and successor, Shimon. Hillel evidently had great confidence in him, as he did in his entire family.[2] We may conjecture that Shimon's reign as *Nasi* was relatively short, since his father's life was long and his son, Raban Gamliel I, also was the *Nasi* for quite a period of time.[3] As we have no sayings or comments of his recorded in the Talmud, he remains an almost anonymous figure. I feel that Shimon's anonymity was of his own making, and certainly not a judgment on his leadership and scholarship. In this respect, he was a worthy successor to his father Hillel, who humbly served without title and without ego as the leader of Israel. There is a tradition that Shimon was martyred by the Romans in the turbulent period leading up to the great rebellion of the Jews in 66 CE. It is also possible that this tradition refers to his grandson, Raban Shimon ben Gamliel I, whose death at the hands of the Romans is on record. However little we know about Shimon ben Hillel personally, it was during Shimon's time that the *Nasi* assumed full control over the direction of Jewish life in the Land of Israel. No longer were there *Zugos*—pairs, equal partners: the *Nasi* became the dominant figure in the Sanhedrin and in the decision-making process of the scholars and rabbis. He was the *mufla sheb'sanhedrin* — the exceptional, chosen leader, the greatest scholar and decisor of the Sanhedrin.[4] And it was Shimon, the son of Hillel, who first achieved this status.

Raban Gamliel I (The Elder)

His son and successor as *Nasi* was Raban Gamliel I (*HaZaken*—The Elder). He was known as "*Raban*"—our rabbi/master/teacher. This is because, unlike previous *Nesi'im*, he no longer had any temporal powers, as Herod's successors and the Romans had generally stripped away all vestiges of communal control from the Jews and their rabbinic leaders. Hence, the title "*Raban*," signifying only spiritual authority.[5] Many illustrious colleagues sat with him on the Sanhedrin of that time (approximately 20 CE). Among them were: Akavya ben Mehalalel; Rabi Chanina Sgan HaKohanim; Raban Yochanan ben Zakai; Shmuel HaKatan;[6] Rabi Eliezer ben Yaakov I; and Rabi Chanina ben Dosa. Each of these great men will also feature in further pages of this book.

Raban Gamliel I lived during a highly volatile period

RABAN GAMLIEL I
c. 10 CE

Teacher
- Raban Shimon ben Hillel

Colleagues
- Shmuel HaKatan
- Akavya ben Mehalalel
- Rabi Chanina sgan HaKohanim
- Raban Yochanan ben Zakai
- Rabi Eliezer ben Yaakov I
- Rabi Chanina ben Dosa
- Chanan
- Admon
- Nachum HaMadi
- Rabi Shimon ish HaMitzpah
- Rabi Myashia
- Zecharyah ben Kavutal
- Abba Shaul ben Batnis
- Rabi Yehudah ben Bseira
- Shimon HaTzanua

Student
- Raban Shimon ben Gamliel I

Relatives
- Father: Raban Shimon ben Hillel
- Son: Raban Shimon ben Gamliel I

Tomb of Raban Gamliel, Beis Shearim

of Jewish history. The new Christian religion had begun and was attempting to usurp traditional Judaism among the Jewish masses. In addition, the relationship between the rabbis of the Sanhedrin and the ruling "Jewish" monarchs of the house of Herod was tense and tenuous. There were also Jewish brigands and criminals who roamed the country, stealing and extorting at will, with little governmental ability to deal with them. And finally, it was becoming apparent that the true rulers of the country of Judea, the Romans, were becoming less and less tolerant of Jews and Jewish practices, thus stirring up great enmity and hostility amongst Jewish nationalists.

Raban Gamliel I attempted to deal with all of these problems with wisdom, tact and efficiency. He assigned Shmuel HaKatan to compose the *Birkas HaMinin*, which effectively excluded Christian attempts to be included in Jewish prayer and synagogues.[7] He adopted a lenient attitude towards the Herodian rulers of Judea in matters of *halachah*[8] and he also adopted a moderate attitude towards the Saduccees as individuals, but not towards their heresies.[9] In general, Raban Gamliel I was a person who was well respected and even beloved by his generation, and especially appreciated by the scholars of Israel.[10] The rabbis therefore saw in his death (approximately 50 CE) the end of an era of honor to the Torah, piety and purity.[11] In grief over the passing of Raban Gamliel I, Onkelos, the esteemed and holy Roman convert to Judaism, burned tens of reams of precious cloth,[12] a custom usually only permitted to mark the death of a king. Onkelos stated that

Emperor Tiberius, Ancient Rome, first quarter of the 1st Century (The State Hermitage Museum)

one Raban Gamliel I was worth more to society than one hundred useless kings![13]

Raban Gamliel I had sensed that the time of the Temple was limited and that therefore the Sanhedrin and its scholars would become the substitute central point of unity and guidance for the Jewish people. He raised the banner of the *Nasi* high, both out of necessity and conviction. The Oral Law was still oral in his time,[14] and to ensure its continuity and authority he strengthened the position and influence of the great rabbinic scholars and teachers of Israel.

He also instituted many matters of public policy that, under his leadership, acquired rabbinic sanction and public acceptance. He followed in the footsteps of his grandfather, Hillel, in initiating policies that he felt were justified to further *tikun haolam*—the improvement and benefit of society at large.

Among these policies were:

- *the establishment of a universal custom of shrouding the dead, wealthy and poor alike, in plain white linen and in preventing drunkenness in the house of the mourners*[15]
- *the formulation of definite guidelines to be used by the Sanhedrin in declaring a leap (thirteen-month) year*[16]
- *the method and manner of acceptance of witnesses, and of the composition of the court itself regarding the "birth" of the new moon*[17]
- *leniencies regarding allowing one witness alone to testify to the death of a woman's lost husband*[18]
- *creating a uniform procedure throughout the Jewish world for writing the names of the spouses involved in a document of divorce*[19]
- *the ability of a widow to collect her kesubah (marriage contract obligations) from her husband's heirs without being forced to take an oath*[20]
- *the reestablishment of the order of the central eighteen-blessing Amidah prayer (Originally formulated at the time of*

"One Raban Gamliel I was worth more to society than one hundred useless kings."

THE ORAL LAW OF SINAI

the Great Assembly, it was now strengthened and reintroduced under the direction of Raban Gamliel I.) [21]

- *clear responses to questions of ritual purity.*[22]

Yet his name is hardly mentioned in matters of *halachah* in the Talmud! Apparently, his opinions and statements are represented in the opinions attributed to the House of Hillel throughout the Talmud.

Raban Gamliel I did not operate alone. On the Jewish scene at that time were many towering personalities, the list of colleagues outlined at the beginning of the chapter being only a partial counting of the early *Tannaim*—the creators of Mishnah. What do we know about them?

Blessing of the moon from Tikunei Shabbat, Germany, 1717 (Israel Museum, Jerusalem)

50

Colleagues of Raban Gamliel I

Shmuel HaKatan—the "small" Shmuel—was called by that name because of his modesty and also to differentiate him from the "great" Shmuel the prophet, the last of the Judges.[23] His lack of personal animosity, even toward enemies,[24] made him the correct choice to compose the *Birkas HaMinin*—the addition to the set *Amidah*, a nineteenth blessing, which separates Jewish apostates, Sadducees, the early Christians and others, from the community of Israel. It is interesting to note that even though Shmuel HaKatan's blessing was accepted and practiced throughout the ages by the Jewish people, Jews still call the *Amidah* prayer *Shmoneh Esreh*—as though it still consisted of only eighteen blessings. Apparently, a negative blessing, justified and hallowed as it may be, nevertheless carries a whiff of disapproval in the collective Jewish soul of Israel.

Shmuel HaKatan's sterling character was exhibited in his willingness to accept personal embarrassment to save others from being shamed.[25] He suffered from many illnesses, but ascribed them to his own moral failings.[26] He was deemed by his colleagues a true disciple of Hillel and worthy to receive *ruach hakodesh*—heavenly revelation.[27] Shmuel HaKatan had no children.[28] His memory was preserved in the Talmud by recognition of his greatness and the enormous sense of loss that his passing created.[29] Since he lived at a time of intense societal turmoil, just before the destruction of the Second Temple,[30] such a serene and holy personality certainly stood out; he was therefore an object of admiration and inspiration.

Akavya ben Mehalalel was also a member of Raban Gamliel I's circle. He was a person of enormous integrity and steadfast character. Because of his scholarship and God-fearing nature,[31] he was offered the office of *Av Beis Din* of the Sanhedrin headed by Raban Gamliel I. However, in order to accept this offer he would be required to recant a number of his halachic decisions, decisions based upon the traditions he received from his teachers and masters. This he refused to do. He is recorded as having said: "Better to be called a fool in this world (for not recanting on his opinions and losing such a prestigious position) than to be seen as doing an evil thing in the eyes of God."[32] There is even an opinion in the Mishnah that Akavya was banned by the rabbis for his stubbornness in not acceding to the opinion of the majority in these instances of halachic dispute.[33] Akavya was spared even more severe punishment for his refusal to accept the opinion of the majority of the Sanhedrin because he never instructed others to follow his opinions; he only stated these opinions in a theoretical fashion, i.e.—*l'halachah aval lo l'maaseh*—in terms of the correct legal interpretation, but not as a ruling to be actually implemented.[34] Akavya is most famous in Jewish tradition for his statement in Avos[35] that one can avoid falling into sinful behavior by constantly remembering where one came from—a drop of semen; and where one is headed—the grave; and before Whom one must give an accounting for the deeds of a lifetime—the Lord God. Akavya is the author of the great rule in life: "*Maasecha ykarvucha, umaasecha yrachukacha*"—by your deeds and behavior will you come closer [to the great rabbis of your time] and by your deeds and behavior will you distance yourself from them."[36]

Rabi Chanina (Chananya) Sgan HaKohanim was a member of one of the last groups of *kohanim* who served in the Second Temple, Rabi Chanina recorded many of his memories regarding the Temple and its service throughout Mishnah.[37] He bitterly lamented the persecution of the Jewish people by the Roman rulers of the country (and by their Jewish agents!) and condemned especially the extortion of Jewish property and wealth by the Roman tax collectors.[38] His public criticism and his independent behavior brought him to the attention of the authorities. His strong opinions and position of leadership rendered him dangerous to the Roman rulers, and he was executed.[39]

He was the link between the generation of those who had served in the Temple and the later generation that no longer saw or experienced the Temple in its glory. As we will see later, the adjustment of the Jewish people to the loss of the Temple was an especially harrowing and traumatic experience. It was the rabbis of the Mishnah who provided the necessary comfort, guidance and hopeful vision to enable the Jews to persevere and survive.

One of the pivotal figures in Jewish history, Raban Yochanan ben Zakai, was a disciple of the great Hillel.[40] In the Talmud, he appears almost as a legendary figure, with a very long life[41] spanning the period of time from the death of Hillel till well after the destruction of the Second Temple. His life overlapped the reign of five of the leaders from the House of Hillel—Hillel himself, Shimon ben Hillel, Raban Gamliel I, Raban Shimon ben Gamliel I and Raban Gamliel II of Yavneh. If I were to describe his life and achievements at this point, I would be getting ahead of myself, chronologically speaking, in the story of the Mishnah and its times. Suffice it to say, that even though he was not a member of the dynasty of Hillel biologically, he was one of the most powerful and influential rabbis during the reigns of Raban Gamliel I and his immediate two successors, Raban Shimon ben Gamliel I and Raban Gamliel II of Yavneh. His disciples span a number of generations and his personal influence dominated a century of Jewish life. A fuller recounting of his life's achievements will appear later in this section, as will the discussion of his disciples.

Tomb of Rabi Chanina (Chananya) Sgan HaKohanim, Galilee

Another colleague of Raban Gamliel I was **Rabi Eliezer ben Yaakov I**. Regarding him the Talmud states: "*Mishnahso kav* *v'naki*"—his teachings are small in number, but pure in content.[42] He is to be distinguished from Rabi Eliezer ben Yaakov II who was a disciple of Rabi Akiva and lived two centuries after Raban Gamliel I and Rabi Eliezer ben Yaakov I.[43] The second Rabi Eliezer ben Yaakov is quoted many times in the Talmud, while Rabi Eliezer ben Yaakov I, as stated, makes relatively few appearances in the Mishnah.

Other colleagues of Raban Gamliel I include Chanan and Admon, two authoritative judges in Jerusalem;[44] Nachum HaMadi;[45] Rabi Shimon ish HaMitzpah;[46] Rabi Myashia;[47] Zecharyah ben Kavutal;[48] Abba Shaul ben Batnis;[49] Rabi Yehudah ben Bseira;[50] and Shimon HaTzanuah.[51]

Raban Shimon ben Gamliel I

After the death of Raban Gamliel I, the position of *Nasi* was filled by his son, Raban Shimon ben Gamliel I. He was the last of the dynasty of Hillel that served as *Nasi* when the Temple still stood intact.[52] His recollections of the Temple service and of the *Succos* rejoicing during Temple times are recorded for us in the Talmud.[53] His father, Raban Gamliel I, had a school of 1,000 students. Half of them studied Torah and the other half were occupied with "Greek wisdom." Raban Shimon recorded that he and only one other from those entire 1,000 students survived the initial Roman destruction of Jerusalem.[54] Until the outbreak of the Jewish war in 66 CE,[55] Raban Shimon and his father had maintained

RABAN SHIMON BEN GAMLIEL I
c. 40 CE
Teacher
Raban Gamliel I
Colleagues
Rabi Yishmael *Kohein Gadol*
Choni HaMaagel
Student
Raban Gamliel II (of Yavneh)
Relatives
Father: Raban Gamliel I
Son: Gamliel II (of Yavneh)

The synagogue at Masada, dating back to the first Jewish revolt against the Romans

THE ORAL LAW OF SINAI

close relations with the Roman government. As matters tragically turned out, Raban Shimon and the last High Priest, Yishmael *Kohein Gadol,* were executed in cruel and painful fashion by the Romans at the conclusion of the war against the Jews.[56]

Raban Shimon is the author of the famous maxim in Avos[57] that the greatest skill in life that he learned from the wise men who frequented his father's house was to be able to remain silent. And true to his maxim, very little is found in the Talmud that is attributed to him. However, he is quoted as the author of the shrewd observation that idleness brings one to boredom and dissoluteness.[58] He is also mentioned regarding a confrontation with the great miracle worker, Choni HaMaagel, regarding adjusting the rainfall in Israel.[59] He is also famous for taking dramatic action to reduce the prices of birds used for sacrifices in the Temple, preventing the dealers from extorting high prices from the public.[60] Martyred and holy, he is remembered in the prayers of Israel on Yom Kippur throughout the ages.

Dedicatory inscription of Pontius Pilate in Latin from the Roman theater in Caesarea, 26-36 CE (Collection of the Israel Antiquities Authority)

The destruction of the Second Temple in 70 CE, and with it the attendant loss of any remaining pretense of Jewish sovereignty over the Land of Israel, created an unprecedented situation in Jewish life. The nascent religion of Christianity was on the rise—claiming to have inherited and replaced Judaism as the faith of monotheism. The surviving Jews had suffered the calamitous loss of national power, and the destruction of their central place of worship. The rabbis were faced with the daunting task of preserving the Torah and the peoplehood of Israel against enormous inimical odds that threatened their demise. There can be no doubt that this successful effort of the rabbis of the Mishnah to preserve Judaism and the Jews after the destruction of the Second Temple was their finest hour and greatest achievement.

It was the Mishnah, and later the Talmud, that served as the lifesaving instruments. The Oral Law, safe from the reinterpretations that Christianity foisted upon the Written Torah, became the national constitution of the Jewish people. Its study, exposition, and values became the norm for Jewish life and existence for all succeeding generations. Jewish life, in essence, became Talmudic life and thus survived and prospered without nation, homeland, Temple, or ruler. There is no other example in human history of such a feat of nation saving, nor of the unaltered preservation of teachings and traditions of millennia, dating yet from Sinai.

> **"I was raised always amongst the wise men and I learned that there is no greater trait for the benefit of the human body than that of silence."**
> *Avos, Chapter 1*

Raban Yochanan ben Zakai

RABAN YOCHANAN BEN ZAKAI
c. 70 - 120 CE
HE LIVED AT THE TIME OF THE DESTRUCTION OF THE SECOND TEMPLE

Teacher
• Hillel

Colleagues
• Rabi Tzadok
• Raban Gamliel I
• Raban Shimon ben Gamliel I
• Raban Gamliel II (of Yavneh)
• Rabi Yehudah ben Bseira
• Rabi Shimon ben Bseira
• Rabi Yehoshua ben Bseira

Students
• Rabi Eliezer ben Hyrkanos
• Rabi Yehoshua ben Chananya
• Rabi Yosei HaKohein
• Rabi Shimon ben Nesanel
• Rabi Elazar ben Arach

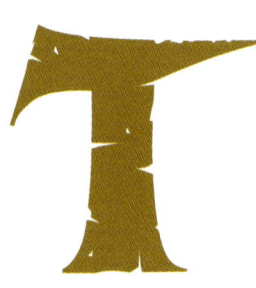

The outstanding hero in this epic story of unlikely Jewish survival is Raban Yochanan ben Zakai. The great Hillel himself described this youngest of his disciples as "the father of wisdom, the father of all later generations."[61] Hillel was confident that Raban Yochanan ben Zakai would be a leading Torah teacher for the Jewish people, and so blessed him.[62] Raban Yochanan ben Zakai lived a long life—120 years, as did Moshe and Hillel and later, Rabi Akiva.[63] Raban Yochanan ben Zakai became a celebrated Torah scholar,[64] though he was originally a merchant by trade. He had devoted himself to Torah study under Hillel, and for the last portion of his life, he was the prime leader and teacher of Israel.[65]

He was a person of sterling character and of prophetic vision. The Talmud attests to his outstanding personal characteristics: He greeted every human being that he saw with kindness and friendship.[66] His *beis din* (court of justice), located in Bror Chayil (in south-central Israel), was noted for its fairness and efficiency.[67] Raban Yochanan ben Zakai searched for all possible ways to implant goodness in society. He made this search for human improvement a key component of his teachings and approach to Torah scholarship. He challenged his students to find the correct way of living and to identify the erroneous paths in life.[68] He was unrelenting in putting into practical effect his realization that Torah alone would suffice to allow Israel to survive.

He was never found without Torah in his heart; nor without *tefillin* upon his arm and head.[69] The first to arrive at the study hall and the last to leave,[70] he greeted each of his students himself at the door to the classroom.[71] He was a master of mental and emotional self-control.[72] He was also known as a miracle worker and as a savant of dreams and supernatural communications.[73]

I believe that when the Talmud describes someone such as Raban Yochanan ben Zakai as being the "youngest" or "smallest" of the disciples of a great person, it implies that this "youngest" person may have been the "last" of the disciples, so to speak. These people, the last ones of an era—such as Shimon HaTzaddik and Raban Yochanan ben Zakai—were people who felt the greatest responsibility for the transmission of Torah from their previous generation of teachers to the coming generation of students, who were the future of Israel.

Above all, Raban Yochanan's traits of realism, coupled with the rejection of false comfort and unrealistic solutions to difficult problems, defined his leadership and behavior. At one and the same time, he was both softhearted and hardheaded. Raban Yochanan knew the world and its pain and evil, the dark side others wished to overlook.[74] He felt the pain of his people as strongly as the devastating personal loss of his own son. He saw Jerusalem in ruins, its citizens reduced to being little more than ghosts of hunger and disease.[75] Death surrounded him, but he came to see death as a stage in life, as a challenge—and even as an opportunity still present for the living.

Citadel of Jerusalem without the walls by David Roberts, R.A., England, 1796-1864, published in 1842 (Library of Congress)

He suffered no platitudes regarding the reality and pain of death. When his son died, his disciples came to comfort him: They told him of the many tragedies that others—great biblical figures—had endured and accepted. However, Raban Yochanan refused to accept the premise that the tragedies of others could somehow provide comfort for him.[76] Only when death itself was explained to him as being a stage in life itself—and that life here on earth was essentially a bailment entrusted to us by our Creator to be returned to Him, and eventually returned again to us—did he find comfort and consolation.[77] He realized that life and death are intertwined, part of the same fabric of human existence, and not separate events. Death seen in the perspective of life itself and eventual eternity has a far different meaning than when being viewed as pure tragedy alone.

That was the lesson he attempted to teach his students by his exercise in initially refusing to accept comfort and consolation over his tragic loss. It is therefore understandable that Raban Yochanan, who understood life and death so profoundly, instructed us on a *misah yafah*—a noble and "beautiful" death: Death with dignity, with the ability to say final words, with a sense of joy and not depression, with clarity of mind, is a noble experience in life's journey.[78] It was all one seamless existence to him. Having bridged that chasm, Raban Yochanan was able to speak not only with the living, but also with the dead.[79] It was not coincidental, therefore, that Raban Yochanan was able to play dead in order to escape from besieged Jerusalem and plead his case for Jewish continuity to Vespasian.[80] To him, life and death were always intermingled and made from the same stuff of Creation.

But Raban Yochanan's greatest trait was his prophetic wisdom and his realistic and practical assessment of conditions and people. He witnessed the destruction of the Temple and saw the coming dispersion of Israel into exile decades before these events actually occurred.[81] Realizing that the Zealots' nationalist cause was doomed, he opposed the war against Rome that began in 66 CE. Dramatic martyrdom and unnecessary unproductive bravado were not his way. He warned against provoking the non-Jewish world and was aware of the dire consequences that such aggressive Jew-

"Grant me Yavneh and its scholars."
Raban Yochanan ben Zakai

ish behavior was likely to bring.[82] His sense of practical realism led him to the conclusion that only by the preservation of Torah study and Jewish practice would the Jewish people be able to endure and survive the Roman onslaught.

When the final siege of Jerusalem by the Roman army of Vespasian began, Raban Yochanan advocated surrendering the city to the Romans, thereby preserving the Temple building and preventing thousands of needless Jewish casualties.[83] The Zealots refused to listen to his advice, stating their confidence in their ultimate triumph over Rome.

Raban Yochanan's conciliatory attitude towards Rome was duly noted by the Romans[84] and helped pave the way for his later successful negotiations with them regarding the preservation of Yavneh and its wise men. He saw what began as a great patriotic struggle against Roman domination degenerate into a bloody civil war amongst the Jews. He was determined to save the people of Israel, even as he realized that no human could now salvage Jerusalem, the Holy Temple and Jewish sovereignty from the clutches of the wild Roman boar.

Abba Sikra, the head of the Zealots in Jerusalem, was a nephew of Raban Yochanan.[85] He initially refused to heed the advice of his uncle and other great rabbinical leaders to surrender the city to the Romans. Instead, he destroyed the ample grain reserves of the city in order to force the Jewish fighters to greater desperation and determination in their struggle against the Romans. But Abba Sikra soon came to realize that the nationalist Jewish cause was lost, and he clandestinely helped his uncle escape from Jerusalem—in a coffin posing as a dead man—in order to plead the case for the Jews to the Roman general Vespasian.[86]

Raban Yochanan made three requests of

Vespasian, Roman Emperor, 70-80 CE (The British Museum)

Vespasian, all of which were granted:

- *Yavneh and its wise men should be spared;*
- *the dynasty of Raban Gamliel should not be persecuted nor executed by the Romans;*
- *medical assistance be provided for Rabi Tzadok, who had fasted for 40 years in anticipation of the coming destruction of the Temple and Jerusalem.*[87]

A later hero of Israel, Rabi Akiva, felt that Raban Yochanan should have requested that Jerusalem be spared.[88] However, Rabi Akiva himself later attempted to overreach in his support of Bar Kochba, to the ultimate despair of Israel. Raban Yochanan, ever the hardheaded realist, understood that such a significant request was unlikely to be granted. He therefore asked only for a *hatzalah poorta*—a "small" salvation.[89] In his wisdom, he knew that this "small" salvation would turn out to be the ultimate eternal salvation of the Jewish people.

When the Roman general, soon-to-be-emperor, Vespasian, granted Raban Yochanan the gifts of Yavneh, sparing the lives of Raban Gamliel's family and the healing of Rabi Tzadok, he inadvertently guaranteed Judaism's triumph over Roman might. The flourishing of Yavneh and its scholars, chief among them Raban Gamliel II and his descendants, helped "cure" Rabi Tzadok's ill-

Coin of "Judea Capta" Aureus (Judea captured) depicting Emperor Vespasian, circa 70 CE

nesses engendered by the pessimism of the destruction of Jerusalem and the Temple. Thus, Raban Yochanan's three requests all had one aim—the preservation of Israel through Torah study and observance.

Raban Yochanan engaged in debate with all of the groups then present in his society. We find him in debate with Romans[90] and other Gentiles, *Tzedokim* (Saduccees)[91] and naturally with many of his colleagues as well—though the nature of the debate with the latter was far different than his discussions with the opponents of Rabbinic Judaism. Many times, in explaining matters of Jewish ritual to non-Jews or to Jewish apostates, Raban Yochanan would dispose of their arguments by "pushing them away with a straw."[92] Not so when he dealt with his students, for then his explanations were based on belief in Torah and the immortal traditions of Sinai—an acceptance of a Jew's duty to perform God's will and commandments.[93]

Raban Yochanan ben Zakai is the bulwark of Oral Law tradition. We find many times in the Talmud that the words of Raban Yochanan ben Zakai are really the words of his mentor, Hillel, who in turn heard them from his teachers, who had heard them from previous teachers until it can be traced back to Moshe on Mount Sinai itself.[94] As a master teacher, Raban Yochanan often pretended to forget, or misstated a matter of *halachah*, in order to encourage his students to develop independent thought, debate and discussion.[95] He is the prime example of the rule in all Torah education that the true teacher must be ready to sacrifice time, honor and personal interests for the sake of educating the students.

His outstanding leadership qualities allowed him to institute almost unilaterally *takanos*—decrees and customs—that became the basis of many areas of Jewish life over the ages. His main purpose in these measures was to preserve the memory of Jerusalem and the Temple in the hearts and minds of Jews forever, and to establish the authority of the rabbis—of Yavneh and its scholars. There are nine *takanos* that Raban Yochanan established to further these goals.[96] Raban Yochanan did not assume the position of *Nasi* permanently, only as a *de facto* status. He saw himself as the caretaker of the office until Raban Gamliel II would return from hiding to assume his rightful place, as the descendant of Hillel, as *Nasi*. When Raban Gamliel II did in fact come to Yavneh—and henceforth was known as Raban Gamliel of Yavneh—Raban Yochanan left Yavneh, the seat of rabbinic authority and the Sanhedrin, and retired to Bror Chayil (probably in the south of the country) where many of his students followed him.[97] He would not allow his presence in Yavneh as the older scholar and the leader of Israel to undermine the role of Raban Gamliel II as the *Nasi*.

This decision was in consonance with the magnanimity of character that proved to be his hallmark.[98] The leader of iron will was also a man of humility, peace and harmony. The recognition of this quality by his contemporaries is what made Raban Yochanan the leader of his generation and the ultimate authority of *halachah* as well as public and diplomatic policy.

His kindness, tolerance, gentility, understanding—and particularly his awareness of the paradox of coexistence of a broad range of people, both great and weak—are reflected in his comments regarding Torah values. Notice how his aphorisms reflect these sensitivities:

- *Fortunate is the generation whose leader admits his errors and brings an atonement for his sins*[99]

- *The stones of the altar which are only inanimate objects, nevertheless one is forbidden to raise a weapon of metal against them to cut them since their purpose is to bring peace and harmony in society, most certainly those humans who strive to bring peace and harmony between spouses, communities, nations and empires will be protected from harm* [100]
- *Why was iron forbidden to be used regarding the cutting of the stones for the altar? Because iron is used to manufacture weapons that shorten human life!* [101]
- *Even the inanimate stones of the altar are not to feel iron touch them, since they bring forgiveness to Israel from its Father in heaven, how much more so shall the Torah scholars of Israel who bring forgiveness to all mankind be protected from all damage and harm* [102]
- *Just as the sacrifice of a Chatas [a sin-offering] in the Temple brings forgiveness for Israel, so too do charitable deeds bring forgiveness for all of the nations of the world* [103]
- *Eliyahu the prophet [at the end of days] will not come to render items pure or impure, to include people or to exclude people [in a wholesale fashion], but only to exclude those who coerced their way [into Israel] and to include those who were pushed away by force* [104]
- *Why was the Jewish slave drilled in his ear by an awl? For his ear heard on Sinai that "You are My servants!" and he went and sold himself to a human master, therefore let his unheeding ear be drilled* [105]
- *God Himself, so to speak, is careful of the personal honor of human beings; [he who steals] an ox that can walk by itself pays five times the worth of the animal [if he slaughtered or sold it] while a thief that steals a sheep [that he must carry on his back] pays only four times the worth of the animal.* [106]

> **"God Himself, so to speak, is careful of the personal honor of human beings."**
> *Raban Yochanan ben Zakai*

Raban Yochanan's decision to move the Sanhedrin and the seat of Jewish authority from Jerusalem to Yavneh was not without controversy. In fact, most of his colleagues disagreed with him and did not follow him to Yavneh. Many of them did not appear in

Yavneh until after Raban Yochanan's subsequent departure in favor of Raban Gamliel II.[107] Many of the scholars could not imagine the survival of Israel without Jerusalem. They could not reconcile themselves to Yavneh or any other place as a fitting substitute for the Temple and Jewish sovereignty in the Land of Israel.

However, Rabi Yehoshua ben Chananya, Raban Yochanan's disciple, remained loyal to him and expressed the forward-looking optimism of his mentor. The Talmud tells us:

After the destruction of the Temple, there were many of the pious who no longer would eat meat or drink wine [symbols of the daily sacrifices offered in the Temple]. Rabi Yehoshua complained to them and said: "If so, my children, let us not eat dates or grapes as well, because they were brought to the Temple as Bikurim [the offering of the first fruits on Shavuos]. Let us not eat bread [brought as a flour offering in the Temple] or drink water [in memory of the loss of the water libation on Succos]." They acquiesced to Rabi Yehoshua in silence.[108]

We are told that Rabi Yehoshua accompanied his master on the road, and from afar they could see the smoldering ruins of the Temple:

Rabi Yehoshua moaned and said, "Woe to us because of this destruction. We have lost the place where the sins of Israel were able to be forgiven." Raban Yochanan replied: "My son, be not dejected. We have another equal means of bringing upon us forgiveness for our sins, and this is through performing acts of kindness and charity to others. For the prophet Hoshea taught us 'For it is goodness and kindness that I desire and not sacrifices.'" [109]

Raban Yochanan's supreme faith and optimism would be sustained for later generations through his loyal and great student, Rabi Yehoshua ben Chananya, as well as his other devoted students.

Concurrent with the Jewish war of rebellion against the Romans in the Land of Israel (and the last years of Raban Yochanan ben Zakai) there were Jewish uprisings against Roman and Hellenistic rule in other parts of the Mediterranean basin. Most of them took place in Egypt, and were concentrated in Alexandria. There, in that most cosmopolitan and developed of ancient cities, the Jews felt themselves oppressed by the majority Hellenists who were supported by the Roman rulers of the city. When the Judean rebellion began in 66 CE, the Romans evidently feared that the Jews of the Diaspora would rise in active support of their brethren in the Land of Israel, widening the rebellion against Roman domination, and they did their best to crush it.

In fact, the Jews of Alexandria did support their fellow Jews in Israel with weapons, money and even some manpower. But their main thrust was to rebel against the domination and oppression of the Greeks and Romans in Alexandria itself. The riots and attacks between the Jews and the non-Jewish groups were fierce, bloody and prolonged. There had been a long history of Hellenistic anti-Semitism in Alexandria, fanned by the notorious lies and calumnies against the Jews published by Flaccus, a Hellenistic scholar of the time. Both Flaccus and Philo (who opposed him),[110] felt they represented the community of Alexandria, and led separate delegations to Rome at the time of Caligula's reign. The emperor verbally abused the Jewish delegation. After decades of strife between the Jews and the Hellenists in Alexandria, the Roman authorities finally intervened forcefully on the side of the Hellenists, and a mass slaughter of approximately 50,000 Jews took place. Tragically, the Roman leader was an apostate Jew, Tiberius Alexander, a nephew of Philo.[111] There is no direct mention of these events in the Talmud, though later rebellions and subsequent persecutions of the Jews in Alexandria, as well as other parts of Egypt and Libya (Cyrenaica), are discussed in the Talmud and will be mentioned later in this book.

Since Raban Yochanan lived a very long life and taught Torah for 40 years, he had many groups of students who studied under him. The Mishnah lists his five main disciples.[112] These five students, Rabi Eliezer ben Hyrkanos, Rabi Yehoshua ben Chananya, Rabi Yosei HaKohein, Rabi Shimon ben Nesanel and Rabi Elazar ben Arach, were from the later group of his students. Rabi Eliezer and Rabi Yehoshua, together with Raban Gamliel II, became the prominent leaders of the Jewish community after the death of Raban Yochanan.

Raban Yochanan died c. 74 CE[113] and after his demise, his disciples who had accompanied him to Bror Chayil now moved to Yavneh to join Raban Gamliel II.[114] However, one of Raban Yochanan's favorite disciples, Rabi Elazar ben Arach, did not join the others in Yavneh but instead moved to a resort town in Syria and came to a sad end there, even forgetting his Torah eventually.[115]

Among the leading men in Yavneh during the lifetime of Raban Yochanan were the three Bnei Bseira—Rabi Yehudah, Rabi Shimon and Rabi Yehoshua—the descendants of the great family that resigned their office of *Nasi* in favor of Hillel. They claimed to have been descendants of the "dead bones" that were revived by the prophet Yechezkel as described in his great vision.[116] Raban Yochanan consulted with them regarding important halachic issues and practices.[117]

This first generation of Yavneh was active in completing *Mishnah Rishonah*—the early or first Mishnah—begun by previous generations, but expanded now to include a description of Temple worship and other issues in danger of being forgotten due to the destruction of the Temple and the loss of Jewish sovereignty in the Land of Israel.[118] This was in line with Raban Yochanan's thrust to create new decrees within Jewish life that would reinforce Jewish memory of the Temple—*zecher l'Mikdash*. But this entire generation—who had yet seen the Temple in its glory and experienced the trauma of its destruction and the Jewish defeat in the war against Rome—was passing on. The mantle of Jewish leadership and responsibility now fell on the shoulders of Raban Gamliel II, Rabi Eliezer ben Hyrkanos and Rabi Yehoshua ben Chananya and their main disciples.

The time was one of great internal and external turmoil and the rabbis of Yavneh were aware of the dangers that hovered yet over their heads. Raban Gamliel II remained a wanted man who survived only by a series of miraculous events.[119] Rabi Eliezer ben Hyrkanos, Rabi Yehoshua ben Chananya and Raban Gamliel II journeyed to

Rome (at great risk to Raban Gamliel!) to seek from Titus himself—who by now was the emperor—a relaxation of Roman oppression of the Jews, if not even a reconciliation. It appears that this delegation first appeared in Rome c. 80 CE.[120] However, Titus was assassinated by his brother Domitian in early 81 CE, and Domitian was much more inimical to the Jews than was Titus in his later life. Domitian even promulgated a decree that demanded the complete annihilation of all Jews living within the Roman Empire. By a miraculous turn of events, the decree expired without ever being enforced. But the distinguished Jewish delegation was never granted an audience with either ruler and they returned to the Land of Israel empty-handed and fearful for the future of the Jewish community there and everywhere in the Roman Empire.[121]

Panel from the arch of Titus, Rome, depicting Roman soldiers carrying looted artifacts from the Jerusalem Temple before its destruction in 70 CE

Rabi Eliezer ben Hyrkanos and Rabi Yehoshua ben Chananya

**RABI ELIEZER
BEN HYRKANOS**
c. 110 CE
Teacher
• Raban Yochanan ben Zakai
Colleagues
• Rabi Yehoshua ben Chananya
• Rabi Yosei HaKohein
• Rabi Shimon ben Nesanel
• Rabi Elazar ben Arach
• Akilas the ger
• Raban Gamliel II (of Yavneh)
Students
• Rabi Akiva
• Rabi Tarfon
Relatives
• Brother-in-law: Raban Gamliel II (of Yavneh)

After the death of Raban Yochanan ben Zakai, Raban Gamliel II of Yavneh was the recognized head of the Sanhedrin and the de facto leader of the Jewish people. However, much of his life was spent not only in fear of Roman execution, as mentioned above, but also in almost constant controversy with some of his colleagues. The two main scholars of the generation, Rabi Eliezer ben Hyrkanos and Rabi Yehoshua ben Chananya, both premier disciples of Raban Yochanan ben Zakai, clashed with Raban Gamliel on matters of *halachah* and policy. Because of these clashes, the internal harmony of the Sanhedrin and its adjacent yeshivah—the *Beis HaVaad* (literally, the meeting house of the scholars)—was badly disrupted. In reality, Rabi Eliezer and Rabi Yehoshua were of two minds altogether regarding aspects of leadership and personal life; and they disputed matters of *halachah* between themselves as well as with Raban Gamliel II.

They were quite different in their life circumstances and mindsets as well. Rabi Eliezer was a man of great wealth through inheritance,[122] while Rabi Yehoshua was a poor blacksmith.[123] In addition, Rabi Eliezer was the brother-in-law of Raban Gamliel II.[124] But in the strict meritocracy of the rabbis of the Mishnah and Talmud, these financial and personal differences played no role.

Rabi Eliezer was a strong and powerful personality. It was not for naught that he was called Rabi Eliezer HaGadol—the Great—by his colleagues. He was great in stature and knowledge, in commitment and service. Nevertheless, like his colleague Raban Gamliel II, he lived a very turbulent life. His Torah education did not begin until he was 22 years old.[125] His father bitterly opposed his leaving the family's farming enterprises and going off to study Torah under Raban Yochanan ben Zakai. Disowned from his share of the family's great wealth, Rabi Eliezer suffered great privation in pursuing his Torah studies, eventually reduced to painful and degrading hunger.[126] Nevertheless, Rabi Eliezer became the premier student of Raban Yochanan ben Zakai.[127] In later years, when his father witnessed his greatness in Torah and the students that flocked to him to study Torah, he offered to restore him to his wealthy inheritance, even at the expense of his brothers.[128] His prowess in Torah knowledge was unchallenged, though his adherence to the rulings of Beis Shammai brought him into conflict with his colleagues and Raban Gamliel II who had firmly established that *halachah* and policy should be based on the rulings and opinions of *Beis Hillel*.

Not only was Rabi Eliezer loyal to the halachic decisions and teachings of *Beis Shammai*, he was similar in temperament to Shammai—strict, strong, unyielding, not given to compromise or giving way.[129] Like Shammai, Rabi Eliezer was not especially welcoming to converts, even to the great Roman convert, Akilas.[130] Fearful that at such a precarious time in Jewish life Rabi Eliezer's policies and behavior could lead to there being "two Torahs" within the Jewish people, the rabbis of Yavneh demanded that he bow to the will of the majority. And true to his firmly held beliefs and strong character, Rabi Eliezer refused to do so. The issue came to a head with the famous halachic discussion that he conducted with Rabi Yehoshua regarding the

"My two arms are like two Torah scrolls."
Sanhedrin, 68a

An ossuary from a collection of Jewish ossuaries, Jerusalem, Herodian period (Collection of the Israel Antiquities Authority)

"oven of *achnaee* (the serpent)."[131] Rabi Eliezer appealed to heaven and performed miracles to support his opinion, while Rabi Yehoshua stoutly maintained the dictum of the rabbis that "the Torah is no longer in heaven," and therefore Rabi Eliezer's ruling is not to be followed since the majority of the rabbis present disagreed with his opinion. Rabi Eliezer refused to accept this contention. Because the principle was deemed so critical at that time, Raban Gamliel II and the others placed a ban of ostracism (*cherem*) upon him. Again, true to his character, Rabi Eliezer nevertheless remained adamant for the rest of his life, never apologizing nor conceding. It was only at his death that the ban was lifted.[132]

Rabi Eliezer's struggles should not be seen as a matter of stubbornness or will between individuals. Rather, he attempted to guide the process of *halachah* according to his teachings and beliefs—and his conviction that the truth of his mentor's teachings took precedence over the will of the majority. He was convinced that "Heaven" agreed with his view. However, those who disagreed with him were equally convinced that *halachah* had to be decided by a majority opinion of the scholars. Otherwise, a unified understanding of Jewish law and practice would not be established. It was felt to be a matter of Jewish survival: Rabi Eliezer was isolated by the scholars in order to preserve the unity of *halachah* and Jewish practice.

Before the ban against him, Rabi Eliezer held a leading role in all public matters regarding the welfare of the Jewish community in the Land of Israel and had already left Yavneh to establish his own yeshivah and court in Lod.[133] As mentioned above, we find that he was a member of the delegation that first visited Rome together with Raban Gamliel II and Rabi Yehoshua a decade after the destruction of the Temple.[134] He also engaged in debate with the early Christians, and as a result found his own life in peril.[135]

In terms of authority, Rabi Eliezer saw himself as more of a partner with Raban Gamliel II in ruling Israel spiritually through the Sanhedrin than as being subservient to him. Perhaps this attitude also exacerbated the relationship that led to the *cherem*. Rabi Eliezer accepted the ban, apparently agreeing that Raban Gamliel II's motives for banning him were pure and just.[136] Nevertheless, the Talmud imputes blame for the apparently premature death of Raban Gamliel II to Rabi Eliezer's sorrow over the ban.[137] Rabi Eliezer continued to teach Torah to his colleagues and disciples even while under ban, though his listeners had to sit some distance away from him.[138]

Apparently, later in his life Rabi Eliezer married his niece, many years younger than he,[139] whom had been raised in his house since she was a child. Though he pointed out to her the disparity in their ages, she nevertheless insisted on marrying him.[140] He lived a long life, and during his last illness all of the great men of Israel came to bid him farewell.[141] On his deathbed, he sensed the persecution that Rome would visit upon the Torah leaders of Israel, and he predicted the fate of his disciples, especially the cruel execution of Rabi Akiva.[142] He bemoaned the fact that though he received much Torah knowledge from his teachers, his students took away relatively little from him.[143] He compared his arms and fingers to scrolls of the Torah itself.[144] It is no wonder, therefore, that upon his death the Talmud records that "when Rabi Eliezer died, a scroll of the Torah was buried."[145]

Like his spiritual mentor, Shammai, Rabi Eliezer was the strong personality of his generation, exacting, uncompromising and unsparing of others in judgment and policy. His will was obeyed in Heaven and he produced many a miracle to justify his cause and opinion. But ironically, through him more than anyone else, the principle was established that halachic decisions are not made in Heaven and that even the greatest of scholars must at times bow to the opinions of his colleagues. The ban placed on him due to his refusal to submit to the majority confirmed this rule of halachic decision. With Rabi Eliezer's final breath, his *tefillin* were removed from him and Rabi Yehoshua, his halachic disputant throughout his lifetime, declared publicly, "The ban is lifted, the ban is lifted!"[146]

Throughout the pages of the Mishnah and the Talmud, Rabi Yehoshua ben Chananya is Rabi Eliezer's companion, as they debated many matters of *halachah* and policy. Rabi Yehoshua served as the *Av Beis Din* in Raban Gamliel II's court in Yavneh.[147] As noted above,

RABI YEHOSHUA BEN CHANANYA
c. 110 CE
Teacher
Raban Yochanan ben Zakai
Colleagues
Rabi Eliezer ben Hyrkanos
Rabi Yosei HaKohein
Rabi Shimon ben Nesanel
Rabi Elazar ben Arach
Raban Gamliel II (of Yavneh)
Students
Rabi Akiva
Rabi Yishmael
Raban Shimon ben Gamliel II

THE ORAL LAW OF SINAI

Rabi Yehoshua was different in temperament, financially poorer and less outspoken than his colleague, Rabi Eliezer. Modest in behavior, Rabi Yehoshua was regarded as the wise man and a leading scholar of his time. Yet, this gentle and humble person, a *kohein*, who like his forefather Aharon loved peace and pursued peace and harmony amongst all human beings, was the center point of great controversies during his lifetime.

From his infancy, Rabi Yehoshua was raised to be a Torah scholar; his mother brought him, while yet in his crib, to the study hall so that the first sounds the infant would hear would be the voice of Torah.[148] Perhaps it was due to his mother's dedication of her son

The tomb of the Sanhedrin, Jerusalem, stone-carved burial cave

to Torah that his mentor and teacher, Raban Yochanan ben Zakai, praised Rabi Yehoshua saying, "happy is the woman who gave birth to him."[149] Raban Yochanan also called Rabi Yehoshua "the threefold cord that will not easily unravel,"[150] alluding to the concept that if there are three generations of Torah scholarship in a family, the family will continue to have Torah scholars in its midst. His colleagues recognized in Rabi Yehoshua a mind that was cleansed from personal agendas or moral weaknesses.[151]

Yet, the circumstances of the time conspired to draw Rabi Yehoshua into bitter controversies with Rabi Eliezer and Raban Gamliel II. Though Yavneh was now the official seat of the Sanhedrin, as a legislative and judicial body it met rarely and sporadically. Viewed by the Romans as a nationalistic body and potentially dangerous to Roman rule, the Sanhedrin was always under Roman scrutiny and pressure. It had to curtail its activities and maintain a very low profile, meeting in clandestine places such as attics[152] and limiting its public pronouncements.

Yavneh instead became the home of the *Beis HaVaad*—the meeting place of the rabbis. At a time when the Sanhedrin could no longer function effectively, clarity in *halachah* and public policy disappeared.[153] Most of the rabbis did not live in Yavneh itself, but traveled there for special meetings and events. In fact, Rabi Yehoshua, who was the *Av Beis Din*, lived in Peki'in, and he, like many other leading rabbis of the time, apparently came to Yavneh only when the situation urgently demanded it.

When we review the history of Yavneh, we see an alarming decline. The first gen-

> "Happy is the woman who gave birth to Rabi Yehoshua ben Chananya."
> *Raban Yochanan ben Zakai*

eration of Yavneh, immediately after the destruction of the Temple, was under the leadership of Raban Yochanan ben Zakai. That special generation clarified *halachos* that were in doubt, edited the first Mishnah that had been compiled at the time of the *Zugos* (three centuries before the Common Era), and enabled Raban Gamliel II to come to Yavneh to restore the leadership of Hillel's family dynasty. It was a time of harmony and rebuilding in Yavneh. However, when Raban Yochanan departed the scene at Yavneh and Raban Gamliel II, together with Rabi Eliezer and Rabi Yehoshua, headed the *Beis HaVaad,* the mood of cooperation and conciliation within the *Beis HaVaad* deteriorated. Though the three made a joint trip to Rome c. 80 CE, as outlined above, these distinguished leaders of Israel soon struggled between themselves.

What caused this critical change of mood from harmony and cooperation to strife and contention in Yavneh? This matter has been debated among scholars for centuries. The Talmud itself is very reticent in discussing these controversies, ascribing technical and legalistic causes to what seems to have been a far deeper fissure amongst the rabbis at Yavneh. I am taking the liberty of interpreting the matter according to the opinions of Halevi,[154] Naftal[155] and Margoliyus,[156] all of whom share a basic premise in interpreting the events recorded in the Talmud regarding these controversies and their causes—though they do not always agree on the understanding of all of the details involved.

The dispute with Rabi Eliezer has already been discussed above. With the banning of Rabi Eliezer, Raban Gamliel II and Rabi Yehoshua remained as the only leaders of the *Beis HaVaad*. When a triumvirate had led the *Beis HaVaad*, matters were more easily settled, for there was always a majority view (two against one) on disputed issues. Rabi Eliezer, who was related by marriage to Raban Gamliel II, and was a long time colleague and personal friend of Rabi Yehoshua—though known for his strong opinions—nevertheless had been able to produce majority rulings that were eventually accepted in the *Beis HaVaad*. With only Raban Gamliel II and Rabi Yehoshua remaining, disagreements arose between them that could not easily be resolved if both stuck firmly to their positions.¹⁵⁷ There would now arise three cases where these two giants of *halachah* would clash, and these halachic disputes eventually led to Raban Gamliel II being temporarily deposed as the head of the *Beis HaVaad* and the Sanhedrin.

The first of their disputes concerned the establishment of the day of Rosh Hashanah.¹⁵⁸ Witnesses testified that the moon was seen on the night of 30 Elul, meaning that Elul was only 29 days long. However, the witnesses also testified that on the next night the moon was not visible. Raban Gamliel II accepted their testimony and proclaimed the first day of Rosh Hashanah to have occurred on 30 Elul/1 Tishrei. Rabi Dosa ben Hyrkanos disagreed, maintaining that the witnesses obviously testified falsely since their testimony was self-contradictory. If the moon was seen on the night of 30 Elul, it certainly should have been seen on the next night as well. He therefore argued that Rosh Hashanah—and hence Yom Kippur—should begin a day later than Raban Gamliel's reckoning.¹⁵⁹ Rabi Yehoshua supported Rabi Dosa's argument against Raban Gamliel's ruling. Raban Gamliel then ordered Rabi Yehoshua to accept the ruling and appear before him with his "money and walking staff on the day that you say Yom Kippur should fall."

Rabi Yehoshua was greatly troubled by this demand. His student, Rabi Akiva, found him in a depressed mood. Rabi Akiva respectfully told Rabi Yehoshua that once Raban Gamliel and his court had decided the matter and acted upon that decision in actually celebrating Rosh Hashanah on 30 Elul/1 Tishrei, there was no going back on that decision. Nevertheless, Rabi Yehoshua further consulted with Rabi Dosa, who in fact had openly criticized Raban Gamliel's ruling. But Rabi Dosa now told Rabi Yehoshua that if the rabbis were to rejudge the decision of Raban Gamliel and his *beis din*, they might be forced to reconsider the judgments of all *batei din* from the time of Moshe as well. In his great humility and in his desire for harmony among the leading rabbis, Rabi Yehoshua obeyed Raban Gamliel's order: he came to him on the day that he had reckoned to be Yom Kippur, carrying his money sack and walking stick. Raban Gamliel rose to greet him and

"A good friend is the most valuable of ways in living human life."
Rabi Yehoshua

kissed him, calling him "my teacher in wisdom and my disciple in accepting my judgment in the matter."

It is interesting to note that Rabi Yehoshua alone was the object of Raban Gamliel's decree, and not Rabi Dosa, who had originated the dispute by publicly disagreeing with Raban Gamliel's ruling. Perhaps, Rabi Yehoshua's role as *Av Beis Din* made him so influential that Raban Gamliel felt that he had to deal with him strongly and publicly; otherwise, there could be two dates for Yom Kippur kept by differing factions of Jews.[160] In any event, this particular confrontation ended peacefully, with Raban Gamliel and Rabi Yehoshua affecting reconciliation between them. However, the memory of this dispute lingered in the hearts and minds of the scholars at Yavneh and within the general public as well.[161]

Most scholars are of the opinion that this dispute centered on the establishment of the limits to the authority of the *Nasi*, who was Raban Gamliel at the time. Once the *Nasi* and his court had decided the matter of the calendar—even if the decision was a faulty one—no one could reverse it. In future decisions regarding the establishment of the calendar, the faulty decision could be taken into account and adjusted, but the decision itself had to stand. Raban Gamliel relied on the tradition that from the time of Ezra onward, the month of Elul never was more than 29 days.[162] Therefore, he accepted the testimony of the witnesses, even if their words appeared contradictory to the astronomical facts. Tradition was to be upheld and the task of the *Nasi* was to do so.

Apparently, Rabi Yehoshua had expressed his support of Rabi Dosa's opinion only privately to Rabi Dosa, but the matter reached the ears of Raban Gamliel[163] and he had to take action. Zealous in protecting the authority of the *Nasi* in order to prevent the very real danger of "two Torahs" arising once again, Raban Gamliel objected to any dissent from his rulings, once they were made, even if said dissent was expressed privately and exclusively to certain individuals. He therefore especially objected to such stated dissent from his *Av Beis Din*, Rabi Yehoshua—for Rabi Yehoshua, who was renowned for his greatness in Torah and sterling personality, was someone about whom a "second Torah" could easily emerge. Rabi

Yehoshua, realizing the national imperative, bowed to Raban Gamliel's wishes in order to preserve the unity of the Sanhedrin and the *Beis HaVaad*.

But shortly thereafter (probably in the same year of the calendar controversy),[164] Raban Gamliel and Rabi Yehoshua again sparred over a halachic issue. A first-born animal (which would normally be brought to the Temple as an offering) from the herd of Rabi Tzadok developed a blemish on its lips while eating. Since the blemish disqualified the animal as a Temple offering, Rabi Tzadok inquired of Rabi Yehoshua as to whether he could slaughter it for regular household meat and hides (*chulin*). Rabi Yehoshua answered that it was permissible to do so. Rabi Yehoshua was aware that the rabbis usually forbade the use of an animal with a self-inflicted blemish as *chulin*, on the grounds that the masses would then purposely inflict a blemish on any first-born animal in order to gain the use of it. (The rule is that a blemish purposely inflicted on such an animal disqualified it from the private use of the animal's owner.) Nevertheless, Rabi Yehoshua told Rabi Tzadok that it was permissible, since Rabi Tzadok was a great scholar and a pious person who was above suspicion of ever trying to circumvent the law. In this stance Rabi Yehoshua was following the opinion of Beis Hillel, which allowed for such differences to be made between Torah scholars and ordinary, less-learned Jews.[165] Raban Gamliel, hearing of Rabi Yehoshua's ruling, which again was made only privately to Rabi Tzadok, strongly disagreed with that ruling. He held, as did Beis Shammai, that no difference was to be made in cases regarding Torah scholars or ordinary Jews.

At a public lecture that Raban Gamliel was delivering, he called out to Rabi Yehoshua, addressing him only by his first name, to stand up and state publicly his opinion regarding this question of whether the *halachah* differentiates between scholars and the unlearned in deciding cases such as the first-born animal of Rabi Tzadok. Asked this question in a public forum, Rabi Yehoshua stated that we do not so differentiate. But Raban Gamliel further challenged him, saying that there was testimony that this statement really was not his position—Rabi Tzadok himself would testify to that. Raban Gamliel did not allow Rabi Yehoshua to be seated as he continued delivering his lecture, despite the fact that the audience was shocked by such public shaming of Rabi Yehoshua, and interrupted the lecture to object.[166]

As tension between the rabbis grew, the stage was set for the final controversy. The debate focused on whether the evening prayer service—*Arvis*—was obligatory or merely voluntary. The Talmud records[167] that a student—Shimon bar Yochai—stood up in the study hall and posed this question to Raban Gamliel II. He had previously discussed the matter with Rabi Yehoshua who had answered him that *Arvis* was to be considered a voluntary prayer. Now Raban Gamliel II answered him, in public, that it was a mandatory prayer. Shimon bar Yochai stated that Rabi Yehoshua was of the opinion that it was voluntary. Raban Gamliel II asked Rabi Yehoshua if there was anyone who disagreed with his ruling that *Arvis* was obligatory. Rabi Yehoshua answered, "No!"

"But I am aware that you personally hold that *Arvis* is a voluntary prayer," responded Raban Gamliel. Once again, Raban Gamliel II made Rabi Yehoshua stand for the remainder of the study session. The students and rabbis, together with others present for Raban Gamliel's lecture, complained bitterly about Raban Gamliel's current and past treatment of Rabi Yehoshua.

Here again, Rabi Yehoshua had given an answer in private to Shimon bar Yochai, who was already noted as being freed of the obligations of prayer due to his extraordinary diligence and exclusive devotion to Torah study.[168] For him, certainly, *Arvis* was not obligatory. However, in public, to the masses of Israel, Rabi Yehoshua would not state that *Arvis* was a voluntary prayer. Raban Gamliel II who disagreed with the premise that an answer in private on a matter of *halachah* could differ from the public stance of the rabbis on the issue, punished Rabi Yehoshua. The other rabbis of the time felt that Raban Gamliel's actions against Rabi Yehoshua were too harsh and unwarranted, and they deposed him from his leadership role as *Nasi* in the *Beis HaVaad*.[169]

Even though Raban Gamliel II was a descendant of Hillel, he was a follower of the rulings and policies of Beis Shammai, as mentioned above. In deposing him, the rabbis sought a way to return to the rulings and policies of Beis Hillel.[170] As that was their intention, they were limited in their choices of his replacement. The appointment of Rabi Yehoshua would be deemed too great an insult to Raban Gamliel II, since he was his antagonist. Rabi Akiva lacked the necessary family pedigree for the role.[171] Rabi Eliezer[172] and Rabi Tarfon were also followers of Beis Shammai.[173] The rabbis therefore chose the young Rabi Elazar ben Azaryah as the replacement for Raban Gamliel II.[174] He was a *Kohein* and a direct descendant of the great Ezra. Scholarly, pious and talented, he led the *Beis HaVaad* through a most difficult and dangerous period in its existence. He convened a special session of the *Beis HaVaad* which almost all of the scholars of the time and their students attended, despite the very real threat of the Roman occupiers destroying the meeting and killing its participants. The Talmud records this event for us and called it *oso hayom* or *bo bayom*—that special, particular day.[175]

In the time of Raban Gamliel's rule, entrance to the study hall and the proceedings of the *Beis HaVaad* was severely limited. Raban Gamliel had posted a guard at the door who was able to somehow ascertain the sincerity of those attempting to enter, excluding those whose "inside did not match their outwardly pious appearance"— *sh'ein tocho k'varo*. Now that guard was removed, and "many more benches had to be added in the study hall." Matters of *halachah* and tradition that had not been definitively decided during Raban Gamliel's reign now were brought up for discussion and decision. The basis for tractate *Eduyos* in the Mishnah was created on "that day." Raban Gamliel himself attended and participated in this extraordinary session, accepting his new role as a participant and no longer the leader of the *Beis HaVaad*. He regretted having excluded so many students from previously participating in the study hall of the *Beis HaVaad*, though he was reassured by Heaven that his policy of strict admissions also had a basis in Torah thought and practice. Everyone was impressed by Raban Gamliel's behavior and his determination to prevent further serious controversy amongst the rabbis.[176] It is interesting to note that Raban Gamliel and Rabi Yehoshua argued once again over halachic matters, but this time the matter was settled and decided in favor of Rabi Yehoshua's position without incident or rancor.[177]

Raban Gamliel personally visited Rabi Yehoshua to apologize for his behavior towards him. Upon entering the home of Rabi Yehoshua, he noticed that the walls of the house were coated in soot and carbon. As mentioned above, Rabi Yehoshua was a blacksmith by trade and the smoke from his fires coated the walls of his dwelling. Raban Gamliel, startled at the condition of Rabi Yehoshua's home, remarked awkwardly: "I see that you are a blacksmith." Rabi Yehoshua answered him in his one and only sharp comment on Raban Gamliel's behavior towards him: "That is the root of your problem, that you are unaware of the private condition, pain and privation of the other scholars [with whom you deal.]"[178]

The two scholars reconciled, and the rabbis of Yavneh now searched for a way to restore Raban Gamliel to his former position of leadership without insulting Rabi Elazar ben Azaryah. They devised a compromise by which Raban Gamliel would hold the position and lead the *Beis HaVaad* for three consecutive weeks and then Rabi Elazar ben Azaryah would assume that role for one week: this cycle would continue indefinitely.[179] Both of these great men accommodated themselves to this pattern, and harmony was restored to the study hall and the *Beis HaVaad*.[180] Nevertheless, the educational and scholarly reforms and decisions that were promulgated on "that day" now remained as part of the structure of the *Beis HaVaad* and as the mainstay of halachic tradition thereafter.

The Heavy Hand of Rome

All of these momentous events described above occurred approximately fifteen years after the destruction of the Temple (c. 85 CE) under the reign of the Roman emperor, Domitian.[181] As the events of "that day" and the streaming of so many new students to Yavneh became known to the Romans, they now suspected that the *Beis HaVaad* in Yavneh was not merely a study hall and religious court, but that it also served as a national rallying center for Jewish independence. Moreover, the greater participation of younger and now strongly assertive figures such as Rabi Akiva, Rabi Tarfon, and Rabi Yishmael in the deliberations at Yavneh served to stoke Roman fears of a new nationalistic uprising by the Jews. Domitian increased the Roman forces garrisoned in the Land of Israel and began a new wave of persecution of Torah scholars, causing them to disperse.[182] Out of the 1,000 highly gifted students of Raban Gamliel II (who were supported by him personally), only two survived the Roman persecutions.[183]

Because of this dangerous situation, the *Beis HaVaad* relocated to the village of Usha in the Lower Galilee. The Sanhedrin would remain in Usha until after the death of Domitian, in the year 96 CE. It was a time of great tension between the Jews and the Roman authorities in the Land of Israel. The Romans suspected the Jews of planning a nationalistic rebellion against them and were diligent in searching for any signs of revolt. To allay Roman suspicions

THE ORAL LAW OF SINAI

and to avoid confrontation with them, the rabbis decided to make changes, even in the order of the prayer services. As an example of the extremes they felt were necessary, the sounding of the *shofar* on Rosh Hashanah was moved to the later *Musaf* (additional) service from its previous position in the early morning *Shacharis*: The Romans would then recognize the blast as part of the continuing worship service and not think it to be an early morning call to arms and rebellion.[184]

But even in Usha, the rabbis did not feel themselves safe from Roman persecution and Raban Gamliel, accompanied by many of the rabbis, moved to Tiberias for a while.[185] While residing in the Galilee, they decided on matters of the calendar year, even though their tradition had been to deal with those matters exclusively in Judah, the southern part of the Land of Israel, close to Jerusalem and the site of the Temple.[186] Raban Gamliel communicated with the members of the Sanhedrin in Usha through secret messengers, though he was upset that important halachic issues were decided there without his presence and consultation.[187]

Ever fearful of capture and execution by the Roman authorities, Raban Gamliel was constantly on the move, despite Vespasian's promise to spare him and his family.[188] Thus the leadership of the Jewish community, which now was entirely based on the scholars and rabbis of the Sanhedrin and the yeshivos, was somewhat shaky. During the years of Domitian's tyrannical reign in Rome, crisis fol-

Site of Cana at Galilee, by David Roberts, R.A., England, 1796-1864, published in 1842 (Library of Congress)

lowed crisis and draconian decrees continued the persecution; rabbinic improvisation and emergency decisions became much more the norm than the exception.

But Domitian's rule in Rome was also shaky. The discontent of the Roman populace with his tyranny and the personal ambitions and jealousies of his own generals culminated in his assassination in 96 CE. In order to avoid a civil war over succession to the imperial throne, a compromise candidate, Nerva, was installed as emperor. This proved to be a wise and sanguine choice. Nerva was a man of intellect and good character, moderate in opinion and behavior, popular with the people and an honest and scrupulous administrator.

He was tolerant of Judaism and Jews and abolished the secret police established by Domitian to spy on the Jews and prevent Romans from converting to Judaism. Though he did not legally abolish the special "Jew tax" instituted by Vespasian, he passively neglected its enforcement. So satisfied was he with his innovative leniency that he even struck a special coin commemorating the non-enforcement of the collection of the "Jew tax."[189]

Because of this change of policy, a second delegation of rabbis journeyed to Rome in order to strengthen the Jewish community there and to effect even better conditions for Jews living in the Land of Israel under Roman rule. The delegation was composed of Raban Gamliel and Rabi Elazar ben Azaryah, the two titular heads of the Sanhedrin and the *Beis HaVaad* now headquartered in Usha, plus Rabi Yehoshua and Rabi Akiva. The latter was already ascending to a role of prime leadership in the Jewish world. The rabbis felt that their mission was of such critical importance that they traveled to Rome on the holiday of *Succos*.[190] And they were, in fact, successful. Many of the decrees against Jewish observance promulgated by Vespasian and Domitian were nullified or non-enforcement was tacitly agreed upon.

While in Rome, the rabbinic delegation found that the Romans were fascinated by Jews and Judaism. Roman aristocracy and intellectuals engaged them in discussions regarding Judaism and its opposition to paganism.[191] The prohibition against conversion to

Judaism was also relaxed by Nerva. In the time of Domitian, people who expressed interest in converting had been persecuted, and even sentenced to death.[192]

Nerva sent his own investigative committee to the Land of Israel to determine if the rumors spread in Rome about Jewish sedition led by the rabbis in Usha were true.[193] The group reported back to Nerva in a manner that was most favorable to the rabbis. Because of this positive development, the rabbis decided to leave Usha and return to Yavneh.[194]

Unfortunately, Nerva was old and sick when he came to power in Rome and his reign was only a little less than two years. With his death, the spirit of tolerance and goodness that he introduced in Roman rule over the Jews dissipated. He was succeeded in the year 98 CE by a Roman general, Trajan, his adopted son. Unlike the wise and gentle Nerva, Trajan was known for his ruthlessness and cruelty.

A general and warrior, Trajan sought to prove his worth as the new emperor by embarking on a new war of conquest against the Parthian Empire, east of Syria and into central Asia. Driven by a fear that a semi-autonomous Judea would be able to threaten his rear supply lines, Trajan determined to destroy the Jewish community in Judea, once and for all. He reintroduced all of the persecutions and decrees of Domitian. The rabbis of Yavneh dispersed once again. At the time, there were two *Nesi'im,* Raban Gamliel and Rabi Elazar ben Azaryah. Perceiving the new danger, they fled to Lod,[195] where Rabi Tarfon had established a yeshivah. Lod was also the residence of Raban Gamliel's brother-in-law, Rabi Eliezer ben Hyrkanos.[196] A tribunal of "five elders" was established there, consisting of Raban Gamliel, Rabi Yehoshua, Rabi Elazar ben Azaryah, Rabi Akiva and Rabi Tarfon.[197]

However, Rabi Elazar ben Azaryah soon left Lod, traveled to the Galilee and took up residence in the town of Tzipori,[198] where he remained until his death. The majority of the rabbis returned to Usha[199] and Raban Gamliel died suddenly in Lod.[200]

Remaining initially in Lod with Rabi Tarfon was Rabi Akiva and his student, Rabi Yehudah.[201] Rabi Chutzpis HaMeturgaman,

Rabi Chalafta, Rabi Yesheivov and Rabi Yosi HaGlili had earlier accompanied Rabi Elazar ben Azaryah to the Galilee.[202] Due to the fact that so many of the sages of Israel were now scattered throughout the land and unable to attend the sessions at Usha, the second convening of the rabbis there was fewer in number and had less authority than the first. In fact, Lod was a counterweight to Usha, with many important rabbinic meetings taking place there under the leadership of Rabi Akiva and Rabi Tarfon.[203]

Because of his youth relative to the other scholars of the time and due to the fear that the Romans would certainly attempt to destroy any descendants of Raban Gamliel, Raban Shimon ben Gamliel II was not immediately appointed to fill his father's role as *Nasi*. Instead, Rabi Elazar ben Azaryah continued to serve, now solely, in that capacity.[204]

Because of the vacuum in leadership and the impossibility of bringing all the rabbis together to set the calendar, we find that Rabi Akiva did something unprecedented: He traveled to Babylonia, within the Parthian Empire (well outside of Roman jurisdiction), to set the calendar and declare a leap year.[205] Returning to the Land of Israel, Rabi Akiva settled in Tzipori, and upon the death of Rabi Elazar ben Azaryah, became the acknowledged head scholar, though he never assumed the official post of *Nasi*.[206] With Rabi Akiva in Tzipori were Rabi Yishmael, Rabi Yochanan ben Nuri, Rabi Chananya ben Tradyon, as well as Rabi Chalafta and Rabi Yesheivov, the latter two having originally accompanied Rabi Elazar ben Azaryah there.

Trajan's anti-Jewish decrees and persecutions[207] eventually provoked a violent Jewish rebellion against Roman rule. The struggle against Roman oppression began in 115 CE, though not in the Land of Israel itself, but in Egypt, particularly in the city of Alexandria. The Jewish community there was large,[208] wealthy, skilled in trades and professions[209] and well armed. The main synagogue in Alexandria was one of the architectural wonders of that cosmopolitan city.[210] But the city was basically a Greek, Hellenistic city, with Jews forming about a quarter of its population.[211]

The relationship between the Greeks and the Jews was one

of envy and derision. Greek anti-Semitism had been strong and virulent since Hasmonean times. Moreover, the inordinate wealth and success of Alexandrian Jewry rankled the Greeks, and they were very competitive with each other in all cultural, religious and economic matters. The emergence of Christianity in Greek society only intensified this antipathy toward the Jews. The Greek population of Alexandria constantly lobbied Rome to enforce anti-Jewish laws and decrees.

With the ascendancy of Trajan to the rule of the Roman Empire, the Greeks of Alexandria erupted violently in anti-Jewish riots. Such riots had occurred earlier in Alexandria,[212] but the Roman rulers of Egypt restored order quickly in those instances. However, in 115 CE a Jewish rebellion began in Cyrenaica (today's Libya) in which the Jews defeated and massacred tens of thousands of Greeks and Romans. This bloody rebellion soon spread to Alexandria, where the Jews took revenge against their Greek and Roman rulers. The initial Jewish successes triggered heavy retaliation from Rome. By 117 CE the violence had ended, but the Jewish communities of Alexandria and the rest of Egypt were decimated. The number of Jewish deaths was staggeringly high, possibly into the hundreds of thousands.[213]

In addition to the rebellions in Libya and Alexandria, there were Jewish revolts—followed by Greek and Roman reprisals—in Lower Egypt, Cyprus and Mesopotamia. All of these events ended in massacres of large numbers of Jews.[214] The Roman general, Julius Lucius Quietus, quickly put down any signs of Jewish rebellion in the Land of Israel in 117 CE. In line with the Roman policy of preventing effective rebellion by destroying the Jewish leadership, the two Jewish lay leaders from Lod, Pappas and Lulianus, were executed.[215]

The relative calm and security of Babylonian Jewry was severely shaken by the events of Trajan's war against the Parthians and his attempted policy of annihilation of the Jews. Babylonian Jewry continued to look for inspiration and strength from the Jewish community in the Land of Israel, a community that was itself embattled and under siege. Nevertheless, in spite of the troubles and problems of Jewish life in the Land of Israel, it remained the center of Torah and Jewish life throughout this second century of the Common Era. Even during the time of Quietus, the great rabbis remained in the Land of Israel, determined to ride out the storm. But the real storm was yet to come upon them.

Trajan died in 117 in Cilicia in the eastern part of Mesopotamia, far from Rome, and in the midst of his war against the Parthians. He was succeeded by his adopted son, Hadrian, a general in the Roman army who had remained at Trajan's side during the war. Hadrian was born in southern Spain and had been orphaned at an early age. Trajan, then commanding Roman legions in Spain, adopted the boy and upon becoming emperor, groomed him to serve as his successor.

Emperor Hadrian, Tel Shalem, Bet Shean Valley, Roman period, 2nd century CE (Collection of the Israel Antiquities Authority)

Surprisingly, Hadrian reversed Trajan's expansionist war policies. He immediately made peace with the Parthians and ceded to them all of the territory conquered by Trajan. He saw himself as the guardian of the status quo of the Roman Empire and shunned any new initiatives to expand its borders. Having studied in Greece, Hadrian was a cultured person and was interested in the arts and philosophy. He was intent on creating a *pax romana* within the Roman Empire itself, striving to address the complaints and correct the injustices perpetrated by his predecessors against the numerous ethnic and national minorities within the empire. He seemed to be the perfect emperor—kind, wise, tolerant, and given to peaceful solutions of disputes and problems.

Hadrian's attitude towards the Jews at the beginning of his reign was most benign, if not even friendly. He removed Quietus from power in the Land of Israel. (Quietus was later found guilty of conspiring to assassinate Hadrian and was executed in Rome. Hillel's words in Avos[216]—"Those that drown you will eventually also be drowned"—again proved to be correct.)

Hadrian even granted permission to the Jews to rebuild the Temple in Jerusalem.[217] A spirit of optimism—even of messianism—swept the Jewish world at this news. However, the Jews fell victim to false reports about their true intentions in rebuilding the Temple. The Samaritans[218] living in Sebastia[219] warned Hadrian against allowing the Temple to be rebuilt, claiming that this would not only have religious ramifications for the Jews, but would have national and military consequences for Rome. Upon hearing this, Hadrian altered his decree regarding the rebuilding of the Temple in such a way as to make it impossible for the Jews to proceed with the work.[220]

Great expectations that are dashed foment deep bitterness and frustration. Hadrian's change of heart regarding the rebuilding of the Temple caused a greater change of heart among the Jews towards him and Rome. The Jews despaired of improving their lot under any sort of Roman domination, no matter how benign. As such, the forces that would bring about another fierce and bloody Jewish revolt against Rome were gathering in Jewish circles.

The immediate threat of revolt was quieted by Rabi Yehoshua ben Chananya, who advised caution, perseverance and acceptance of the reality of Roman power and rule.[221] In spite of Hadrian rescinding permission to rebuild the Temple, the rabbis felt that overall Roman policy towards the Jews was now more favorable than it had been for decades. They moved back again to Usha in the Galilee and there re-established the Sanhedrin.[222] It had been twenty years since they had left Usha to return to Yavneh. The survivors of the Sanhedrin in Yavneh were Rabi Yehoshua, Rabi Akiva and Rabi Yishmael. Rabi Yehoshua was now very old and did not come to Usha.

Rabi Akiva

Rabi Akiva became the effective head of the Sanhedrin, and his colleagues and disciples now gathered around him there.[223] He did not serve as the *Nasi*, a role reserved for, but not yet filled, by Raban Shimon ben Gamliel II, the son of Raban Gamliel of Yavneh. He was rather the *Av Beis Din* and the leader of the yeshivah in Usha. Raban Simon ben Gamliel II was called "the son of the *Nasi*," but was not publicly appointed *Nasi* out of continuing fear of the Roman authorities' enmity to the official leaders of the Jews.

Joining Rabi Akiva at Usha were his colleagues and students, including Rabi Chanina (Chananya) ben Tradyon, Rabi Elazar ben Parta, Rabi Yosi HaGlili, Rabi Yehudah bar Eelai, Shimon ben Azai, Rabi Yesheivov HaSofer, and Rabi Yochanan ben Nuri. The decrees and public policies created by these scholars are called *takanos Usha*—the decrees promulgated at Usha.[224] But the glory days at Usha were short-lived this second time as

RABI AKIVA
c. 135 CE

Teachers
- Rabi Eliezer ben Hyrkanos
- Nachum ish Gamzu
- Rabi Yehoshua ben Chananya
- Raban Gamliel II

Colleagues
- Rabi Tarfon (he originally was his teacher)
- Rabi Yishmael
- Rabi Chanina (Chnanaya) ben Tradyon
- Raban Shimon ben Gamliel II
- Rabi Elazar ben Parta
- Rabi Yosi HaGlili
- Rabi Yehudah bar Eelai
- Shimon ben Azai
- Shimon ben Zoma
- Elisha ben Avuyah (Acher)
- Rabi Yesheivov Hasofer
- Rabi Yochanan ben Nuri
- Rabi Dosa ben Hyrkanos
- Rabi Yehoshua ben Levi

Students
- Rabi Meir
- Rabi Nosson
- Rabi Shimon ben Yochai
- Rabi Elazar ben Shamua
- Rabi Yehudah ben Bava

Relatives
- Sons: Rabi Yehoshua ben Korcha, Shimon ben Akiva, Asa (Isai) ben Akiva, Chananya ben Akiva, Chama ben Akiva
- Sons-in-law: Shimon ben Azai, Rabi Yehoshua ben Kapusai

Tomb of Rabi Akiva ben Yosef, interior, Tiberias

well. The influence of the Hellenist anti-Semites was taking effect on Hadrian.

He was determined to solve Rome's "Jewish problem" finally and decisively. Instead of allowing the Jewish Temple to be rebuilt in Jerusalem, Hadrian decreed that Jerusalem should be leveled to the ground and upon its ruins would be built a purely pagan Roman city, Aelia Capitalina. He constructed a temple to Jupiter on the Temple Mount, over the ruins of the destroyed Jewish Temple.[225] His decrees included forcing the Jewish population of Jerusalem to leave the city and banning circumcision.[226] All Jewish appeals to the emperor and to his advisers to ameliorate the situation were rebuffed.

Hadrian himself was in the Land of Israel in 131 CE and the Jews appealed directly to him to soften his enmity against them. When he left to return to Rome in 132—without addressing any of the issues raised by the Jews—a bitter wave of resentment against Rome swept through the Land of Israel. The stage was now set for the bloody revolt of the Jews, led by Shimon ben Kosiba (Bar Kochba), against Roman rule.

The main figures leading the Torah world at this time were Rabi Tarfon, Rabi Akiva and Rabi Yishmael. Rabi Akiva was not only the dominant scholar and leader of his time; his personality lives on, influencing all future Jewish generations as well. He is the spirit of the undying power of Torah within the Jewish people, of the goodness and kindness of Judaism, and of the tenacity and optimism of Israel in the face of the most horrendous of enemies and circumstances. The Talmud[227] tells us that when Rabi

Seal of the 10th Roman Legion Fraternis, which took part in the conquest of Jerusalem

Dosa ben Hyrkanos, the elder sage of his day, first met Rabi Akiva, he said to him, "Are you Akiva ben Yosef, whose great name extends from one end of the world to the other end?" Perhaps Rabi Dosa was not only referring to the world of his time, but to the eternal world of the Jewish people as well. Rabi Akiva's name and presence, his wisdom and hope, walk with all of the Jewish people throughout all of our history—from one end of our world to the other end—in all times and in all places.

In the chain of the Oral Law that extended from Moshe to Ezra to Hillel to Raban Yochanan ben Zakai to Rabi Eliezer and Rabi Yehoshua, Rabi Akiva became the unbreakable link, binding Israel to Sinai and to the covenant of Torah. Perhaps more than all of the great men of the Mishnah, he became the primary symbol of Torah greatness, and of love of the Jewish people[228] and all mankind. It is not by chance that when Moshe asked God, so to speak, why there were crowns being attached to the letters of the Torah, the reply he received was that Rabi Akiva would someday use them to interpret the Torah.[229] It is no exaggeration to say that Rabi Akiva is himself the crown on the letters of the Torah for all of the Jewish people for all ages.

Tradition compares Rabi Akiva's long and eventful life span to that of Moshe Rabeinu, who lived 120 years.[230] It also suggests that he was a convert,[231] or at least from a family of converts, for he is reported in the Talmud to be a descendant of Sisera, the Canaanite general slain by Yael.[232] He was alive and already well known at the time of the Temple's destruction[233] in 70 CE and was executed by the Romans c. 135 CE. During his youth[234] he was an uneducated shepherd, employed by Kalba Savua, one of the wealthiest Jews of the era immediately preceding the destruction of the Temple.[235] He was not only unlettered in Torah, but he possessed within him an irrational hatred towards Torah scholars.[236] In one of the more remarkable personal stories recorded in the Talmud, we are told that Rachel, the daughter of Kalba Savua, eloped with Rabi Akiva and sent him away to learn Torah for many years.[237]

Rabi Akiva studied with Nachum Ish Gamzu,[238] Rabi Eliezer and Rabi Yehoshua.[239] It is clear that he was also a student of Rabi

"Tradition is the fence that protects Torah; tithing to charity is the fence that protects wealth; silence is the fence that protects wisdom."
Rabi Akiva

Tarfon, who later was regarded as his colleague.[240] His prodigious accomplishments in his Torah studies allowed him to rather soon become a colleague of his teachers[241] and he then conducted a yeshivah of his own, comprised of thousands of students.[242] He ascribed all of his Torah greatness and accomplishments to the encouragement of his beloved wife, Rachel.

After Rabi Akiva's fame was known, Kalba Savua reconciled with his daughter and son-in-law and made Rabi Akiva a wealthy man.[243] He remained wealthy all of his life, with various fortunes falling to his lot over his lifetime.[244] Rabi Akiva respected wealth and people of wealth,[245] yet he became the champion of the poor, perhaps because of his great wealth, or because he had known the bitter sting of poverty in his own life. The Talmud refers to him as being "the collector of money for the poor"[246] for when he felt that a wealthy person, such as Rabi Tarfon, did not contribute sufficiently to charity for the poor, he took measures to convince him to be more charitable.[247] People left money to Rabi Akiva upon their death, confident that he would properly distribute their wealth to charitable purposes.[248]

Though we have no full description of the physical appearance of Rabi Akiva, we do know that he was quite tall[249] and that he was bald.[250] Rabi Akiva maintained a large yeshivah in Bnei Brak, his main home and base[251] when he was not participating in the deliberations of the Sanhedrin and the scholars in Yavneh or Usha. The teacher of many thousands of students,[252] he is seen as the pivotal individual in the development of the Oral Law after Hillel and Raban Yochanan ben Zakai. The development of Mishnah,[253] *Sifra, Sifrei, Mechilta, Tosefta*, and all of the other works of the Oral Law of the time, was based completely on Rabi Akiva and his students.[254]

In effect, Rabi Akiva brought order to the myriad laws and traditions of the Oral Law. He fashioned the Oral Law into "rings and rings"[255] that could now be handled, remembered and studied more easily. Since Rabi Akiva lived a very long life there are several generations—three, or perhaps, even four—of his disciples who carried forward the study of Torah and the development of the Oral Law. His last disciples—Rabi Meir, Rabi Yehudah bar Eelai, Rabi

Nechemiah and Rabi Shimon bar Yochai—are best known to us in these endeavors. However, the earlier students of Rabi Akiva were, in fact, the teachers and mentors of the latter students; so the Talmud rightfully states that for a century of Jewish learning and Torah scholarship "all was according to the methods and teachings of Rabi Akiva."[256]

No area of Torah was left untouched or unrefined by Rabi Akiva's comments and opinions. Even when some of his original teachers, such as Rabi Elazar ben Azaryah and Rabi Yosi HaGlili, chastised him for commenting on matters of *Aggadah*[257] and told him to stick to matters of *halachah*,[258] Rabi Akiva never flinched from expressing his ideas and interpretations on all Torah matters.[259] This trait did not prevent Rabi Akiva from being humble and modest. Ever wary of the danger of "two Torahs," he never insisted on his opinion becoming law when that opinion was contradicted by more than one other scholar; and he bowed to their judgment and did not practice his own opinion, even though he felt it to be the correct one.[260] Thus the Talmud ruled that Rabi Akiva's opinion is always to be followed if the discussion is only between him and one other scholar, but if the discussion is between him and more than one other scholar, Rabi Akiva's opinion is not to be followed—for he himself would not go against the wishes and opinions of a majority of his fellows.[261] There is an opinion in the Talmud that Rabi Akiva's greatness was of such magnitude that his opinion would be followed even if it conflicted with the opinion of his own teacher and mentor![262] Rabi Tarfon summed up the attitude of his colleagues towards Rabi Akiva when he said, "Akiva, [when] anyone separates and leaves you, it is as though he separates and leaves life itself."[263]

First Hebrew Shekel, 66 CE (Israel Museum, Jerusalem)

THE ORAL LAW OF SINAI

Rabi Akiva is famous in the Talmud for having his prayers on behalf of Israel answered.[264] His effectiveness in channeling God's mercy was attributed to his own special humility and pliability in regard to others.[265] Perhaps his most famous personal trait was his unflagging optimism regarding himself and the future of the Jewish people.[266]

This consistent and eternal optimism was strong despite much personal tragedy and disappointment in his lifetime. He had five sons: Shimon, Chananya, Chama (Chanina), Asa (Isai) and Yehoshua[267] as well as a number of daughters. Among his sons-in-law were the prominent Shimon ben Azai[268] and Yehoshua ben Kapusai.[269] Tragically, however, a number of his children died during Rabi Akiva's lifetime.[270] He took comfort in the crowd that came to comfort him on the death of his son Shimon, and in the fact that Shimon's public good deeds would bring him into the eternal life of the World to Come.[271]

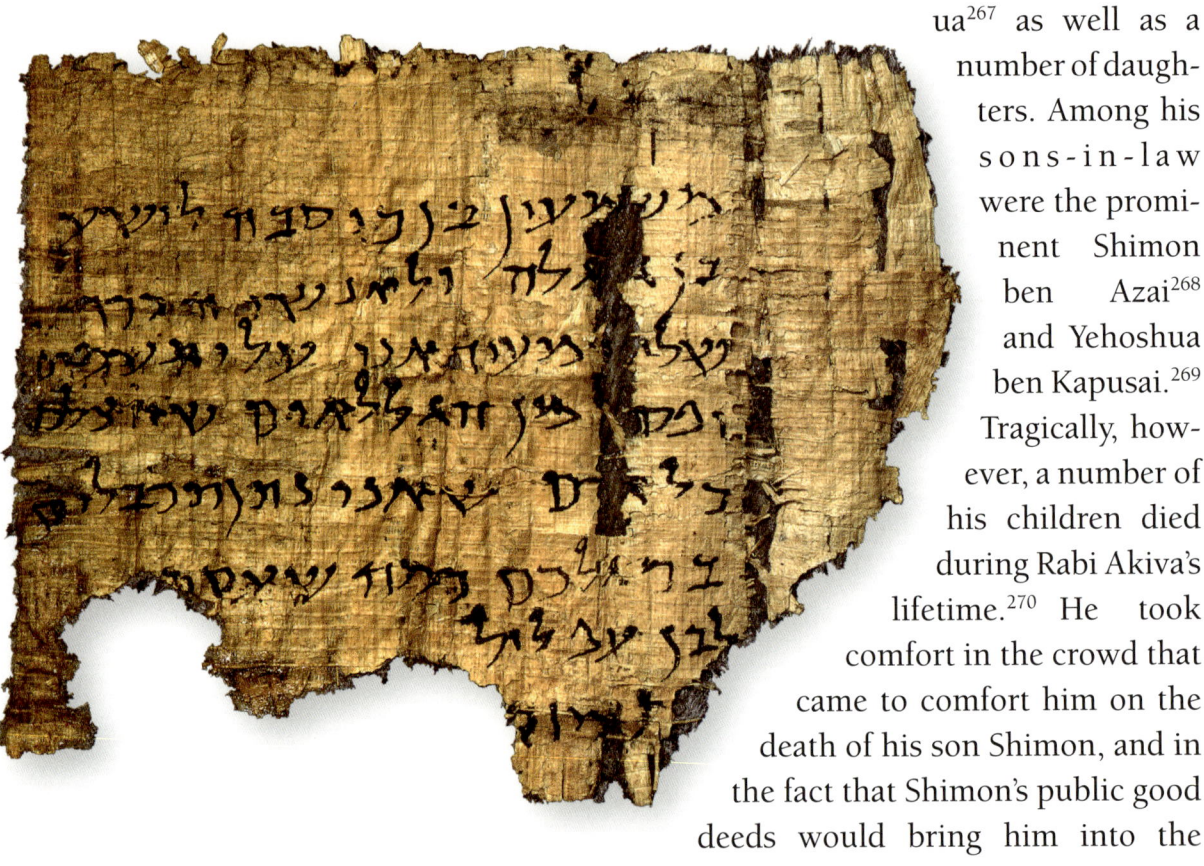

A letter from the collection of Bar Kochba Letters, Nahal Hever, circa 132-135 CE (Collection of the Israel Antiquities Authority)

To support the various Jewish communities and to win concessions for the Jewish people from the Roman authorities, Rabi Akiva traveled widely. It is known that he journeyed to Arabia and Africa,[272] Asia Minor,[273] Antioch,[274] Rome,[275] Media/Persia[276] and "the cities of the sea."[277] Though his life was endangered by these missions,[278] he continued them even into his old age. His devotion to the Jewish people knew no limits and his personal sacrifices on its behalf were legendary. He dealt with the Roman authorities on a regular basis and was well known and respected by them, even though he was a thorn in their side.[279]

One of the more ironic aspects of his legendary life was that in his later years, after he was widowed, he married the widow of Tinnaeus Rufus, the infamous Roman governor of Judea. She had converted to Judaism after the death of her husband and had helped support Rabi Akiva and his work.[280] His remarkably dynamic and productive life would end tragically at the hands of the Romans, as will be discussed later in this chapter.

Rabi Akiva's role in the revolt against Rome is both lofty and disastrous. After the disappointments regarding Hadrian's change of heart towards the Jews, zealous Jewish nationalists arose and demanded war against Rome to expel their troops from Judea. They were led by Shimon ben Kosiba, popularly known as Bar Kochba. An analysis of Bar Kochba's rebellion is not our concern here,[281] but rather Rabi Akiva's involvement in it. He not only supported Bar Kochba and his rebellion against Roman rule—Rabi Akiva actually declared Bar Kochba to be the Messiah of Israel![282]

Such a pronouncement from the great Rabi Akiva no doubt raised the hopes of the populace and encouraged thousands to flock to Bar Kochba's army. Yet most of his colleagues disagreed with him, aptly expressed by Rabi Yochanan ben Torta: "Akiva, grass will grow from your cheeks and still the Messiah, the descendant of David, yet will not have come!"[283]

The rebellion met with initial success, as Bar Kochba forced the Romans to abandon Jerusalem. He even began to restore the ruins of the Temple and struck coins for the new Jewish state. His reign, however, was for only two and a half years,[284] as the Romans rallied and reinforced their armies. Soon, Bar Kochba and his men were besieged in Beitar; and when the city succumbed to the superior Roman might, the Romans enacted a fearful slaughter of its inhabitants.[285] Rabi Akiva had lost faith in the revolt even before the final fall of Beitar. Bar Kochba's bitter disputes with leading rabbis and his execution of his uncle, Rabi Elazar HaModai, one of the great scholars of the time, proved him to be no Messiah.[286]

> "Akiva, anyone who separates and leaves you, it is as though he separates and leaves life itself."
> *Rabi Tarfon*

It is noteworthy that Rabi Akiva's reputation and standing amongst his colleagues and the people did not suffer in spite of Bar Kochba's failure. Such was his stature and greatness—that even his error in declaring Bar Kochba the Messiah of Israel was overlooked! His unflagging optimism in the face of all tragedies and disappointments triumphed over the reality of Bar Kochba's defeat.[287] Thus Rabi Akiva became the symbol not only of Jewish martyrdom but, perhaps more importantly, of Jewish faith and hope.

After the fall of Beitar, the Roman authorities were determined to quench the fire of Jewish rebellion once and for all time. Recognizing that the flame of Jewish nationalism was fueled by religion, they began a systematic persecution of the religious leaders of Jewry and banned the public teaching of Torah. Rabi Akiva defied this ban and continued his public discourses on Torah,[288] justifying his course of action with the premise that the Torah is the basis for Jewish existence: therefore not teaching Torah would be tantamount to national suicide.[289] Arrested by the Romans and placed in prison,[290] Rabi Akiva somehow continued to teach Torah to his disciples who were permitted to visit with him.[291] Before his arrest, he was able to travel to the south of Judea and there he transferred the leadership of the coming generation to Rabi Meir, Rabi Yehudah bar Eelai, Rabi Shimon bar Yochai and Rabi Elazar ben Shamua.[292]

Now, in prison and awaiting a horrifying execution, he continued to teach and encourage the Jewish people. Ever the optimist, he saw past the terrible times of Roman persecution and envisioned the redemption of the Jewish people![293]

Tradition, immortalized in the *Selichos* prayer of Yom Kippur *Minchah* and the *Kinos* of Tishah B'av, records that Rabi Akiva was tortured to death, his skin flayed by iron combs, on Yom Kippur eve[294] and expired with the words of *"Shma Yisrael"* on his lips.[295] He told his stu-

Bar Kochba coin, Tetradrachm ("Sela" in Hebrew) 132–135 CE (Israel Museum, Jerusalem)

dents that he looked forward all of his life to martyrdom in order to fulfill the commandment of loving God with all of one's life—even when one's life is being taken.²⁹⁶ The place designated for Roman executions of the time was in the amphitheater or the hippodrome of Caesarea. However, there is an opinion that infers that Rabi Akiva may have died of natural causes while in prison on Erev Yom Kippur.²⁹⁷ Tradition also has it that Rabi Akiva was buried in Tiberias, though Midrash states that he was interred in Antipras, a city named by Herod for his father, Antipater. It is said that a special cave miraculously opened to house Rabi Akiva's earthly remains.²⁹⁸

But to the Jewish people, Rabi Akiva does not remain buried in his grave. He lives on. In all generations of Jews, his hope and confidence in our bright future comforted Israel through the long night of exile. He lives on in the study halls of Torah that immortalize his name, his *halachah* and his life, and in the hearts and minds of all Jews who daily recite *"Shma Yisrael."*

SECTION III
RABI MEIR TO RABI YEHUDAH HANASI
C. 140 CE - 200 CE

Palestine, the tribes, and Jerusalem
(La Palestine, les tribus, et Jerusalem)
by Jean Baptiste Bourguignon d'Anville,
1697-1782, published ca. 1783
(Library of Congress)

The End of an Era

As described previously, after the fall of Beitar, the Romans exacted full revenge upon the Jews of Judea, and we therefore find references to the destruction and eventual restoration of the cities of Judah throughout the Talmud.[1] Hadrian's fury was not restricted to destroying cities and uprooting Jewish communities in Judea:[2] He was determined to destroy the religious leadership of the Jews as well as the observances of the Jewish faith. The decade following the Bar Kochba rebellion—which ended c. 148 CE—is known as the time of *shmad,* of forceful coercion to desert Judaism. Jews were tortured and executed for observing the commandments of the Torah,[3] and many of the great scholars were martyred.[4]

Surprisingly, the Romans were helped in their attempt to destroy Judaism by Jews—some of whom apparently had been Torah scholars themselves![5] There are those who say that it was during this period of *shmad* that the early Christians in the Land of Israel abandoned completely their previous tenuous identity with the Jewish community, and from this time forward Christianity severed its ties to Judaism and the Jewish people.[6] In any event, the era of *shmad* was one of the most

Emperor Antoninus Pius

severe tests of the loyalty of the Jews to Torah and to observance of ritual.[7]

One of the martyrs of Israel at this time was Rabi Yehudah ben Bava: He defied the Roman ban on granting *semichah* (ordination to serve on the Sanhedrin) by ordaining five of the outstanding disciples of Rabi Akiva. Though he paid for this act with his life, his brave act preserved the chain of tradition and rabbinic authority, the very lifeblood of Jewish existence and long-term survival.[8] The five rabbis were Rabi Meir, Rabi Yehudah bar Eelai, Rabi Shimon bar Yochai, Rabi Yosi and Rabi Elazar ben Shamua. There is an opinion in the Talmud that Rabi Nechemiah also was ordained then.[9] Rabi Akiva himself placed the burden of Jewish leadership on these scholars in his own lifetime, and he appointed Rabi Meir to be the head of the group.[10] He intended to ordain Rabi Meir, but it was not until after Rabi Akiva's death that Rabi Meir accepted ordination.[11] As Rabi Yehudah ben Bava was granting ordination, he saw Roman soldiers coming hard upon them, brandishing spears. Mortally wounded, his final instruction to these precious new leaders of Israel was: "Flee, my sons, flee!"[12]

Tomb of Rabi Yehudah bar Eelai, Ein Zeitim between Tzfat and Meron

There is an opinion that these great rabbis then fled from Roman control to Babylonia, at that time part of the Parthian Empire, where they found refuge with Rabi Yehudah ben Bseira in Peki'in.[13] The Torah community in the Land of Israel remained underground and desolate until after the death of Hadrian.

The hated emperor passed from the scene c. 138 CE and was

succeeded by Antoninus Pius.[14] After solidifying his reign, Antoninus relaxed the decrees of Hadrian against the Jews. Rabi Meir and his colleagues returned to the Land of Israel in c. 143 CE. Their immediate and pressing task was the fixing of the calendar and its attendant leap years. In an emergency meeting held in Bikas Rimon, they dealt with these calendar issues and settled them "with a kiss to each other,"[15] i.e. that even when they differed with each other in matters of *halachah* and policy, these rabbis of the Mishnah respected and loved each other.

They now attempted to restart the Sanhedrin and with it the main yeshivah of Torah study in the Land of Israel. Apparently, even under the more relaxed rule of Antoninus Pius, a return to Yavneh and Judea still was deemed too dangerous, so they once again turned to Usha in the Galilee. From their base there, the rabbis issued a call for all of the scholars to congregate in Usha.[16]

Yet the harshest of Hadrian's decrees against Judaism had still not been repealed: Sabbath observance, circumcision and observance of the laws of family purity were still forbidden. The rabbis in Usha now attempted to have these decrees annulled by sending a delegate to Rome to argue their case to the emperor. They chose Rabi Reuven ben Eetzrebuli.[17] His attempt to convince the Roman authorities of the benefit that would accrue to the government in lifting those anti-Jewish decrees failed. The rabbis did not despair, and sent a second delegation composed of Rabi Shimon bar Yochai and Rabi Elazar ben Rabi Yosi. With the help of a supernatural event, this delegation was successful in having the decrees annulled.[18] The visit to Rome, and what he saw there of Roman society, soured Rabi Shimon bar Yochai on all aspects of Roman culture and achievements. Even as the relaxations of the laws against Judaism proceeded apace, the gulf of mistrust between the Romans and the Jews remained wide.

The Talmud records the conversation between Rabi Yehudah, Rabi Yosi and Rabi Shimon bar Yochai regarding their differences on what should now be the proper attitude toward the more moderate behavior of the Romans in the Land of Israel. It seems obvious that after destroying most of Judea, the Romans now began to rebuild it, albeit in Roman style and detail and undoubtedly for the gain of their empire. Nevertheless, Rabi Yehudah praised the Roman efforts at rebuilding the country as being worthy of appreciation and gratitude. Rabi Yosi remained silent, reflecting his ambivalence and doubts as to Rome's true intentions. Rabi Shimon bar Yochai was vocal and vehement in his criticism of the Romans, stating that everything they did, even if seemingly positive on the surface, was truly impelled by an evil agenda and selfishness. The conversation was overheard by Yehudah ben Gerim[19]—a Jewish scholar apparently of Roman ancestry—who reported it to the Roman authorities. The Romans thereupon rewarded Rabi Yehudah; exiled Rabi Yosi to Tzipori, a mixed Roman-Jewish community where he would be under Roman surveillance; and marked Rabi Shimon bar Yochai for death.

Rabi Shimon and his son, Rabi Elazar ben Shimon, fled to the Judean desert (legend has it that they went to Peki'in in the Galilee), where they miraculously survived by hiding in a cave for thirteen years.[20] It was during this time that Rabi Shimon perfected his holiness, as will be discussed later in this section.

The story in the Talmud of the discussion between the rabbis[21] reflects the differing currents of thought then prevalent in Jewish life. How best to reestablish the Jewish community after the relaxation of Hadrian's decrees was no easy matter.

The rabbis of Usha had great respect for the city of Yavneh, since it was the location of the original salvation of Torah by Rabi Yochanan ben Zakai after the destruction of the Temple. It had been the *achsanya*—the welcoming house and Torah oasis in terrible times.[22] They felt it was time to renew the Torah center at Yavneh, even if not all of the rabbis would be able to return there. The meeting at Yavneh had to be kept low profile, so as not to antagonize the Roman authorities. Despite the quiet, clandestine planning of the proposed meeting, the Romans established checkpoints on the road to Yavneh to limit the number of rabbis arriving there.[23]

At the meeting, the rabbis who had managed to get there instituted a special concluding blessing to *Birkas HaMazon*—the Grace after Meals.[24] This blessing, in memory of the martyrs of Beitar and the Bar Kochba rebellion, was in thanksgiving for the fact that the Jews massacred by the Romans eventually came to Jewish burial and that their bodies had not decayed until that burial took place. The institution of such a blessing was in itself an act of subtle defiance against the Roman authorities, indicating that Rabi Shimon bar Yochai's assessment and indictment of Rome and its motives had wide popular support among the rabbis at Yavneh.

The convocation of the rabbis at Yavneh was not of long duration. The *Nasi*, Raban Shimon ben Gamliel II, was not present, apparently out of fear of the Roman authorities.[25] The attempt to renew the Sanhedrin at Yavneh was thus unsuccessful and the center remained at Usha.

Tomb of the Tanna, Rabi Shimon Bar Yochai and his son Rabi Elazar, Mount Meron

But even Usha was not a safe place for them. Since the Sanhedrin had already met there once before, the Romans were likely to monitor intensively their deliberations. Therefore, the rabbis moved to a smaller community in the Galilee with no previous history of hosting a Sanhedrin—Shfar'am,[26] a location not far from Usha and Tzipori, the main centers of Jewish population in the Galilee at the time. When the rabbis reconvened at Shfar'am, Rabi Meir was the *Chacham*—the acknowledged leading scholar of the group[27] and Rabi Nosson HaBavli was the *Av Beis Din*.[28]

Rabi Meir

RABI MEIR
c. 150 CE

Teachers
- Rabi Akiva
- Rabi Yehudah ben Bava
- Rabi Chanina (Chananya) ben Tradyon
- Elisha ben Avuyah (Acher)

Student
- Sumchos

Colleagues
- Rabi Nosson
- Rabi Yehudah bar Eelai
- Rabi Shimon bar Yochai
- Rabi Elazar ben Shimon
- Rabi Shimon ben Gamliel II
- Rabi Elazar ben Shamua
- Rabi Yehoshua ben Korcha
- Rabi Yochanan HaSandlar
- Rabi Yaakov ben Korshai
- Rabi Yehoshua ben Levi
- Rabi Eliezer ben Rabi Yosi HaGlili

Relative
- Father-in-law: Rabi Chanina (Chananya) ben Tradyon

Rabi Meir is one of the most gigantic, enigmatic and yet pivotal figures in the story of the creation of the Mishnah. His was a personal life of tragedy and upheaval; but it was also a life of great sacrifice, holiness and enormous accomplishments.

Tall in physical stature,[29] Rabi Meir was descended from a Roman convert, a close relative of the Emperor Nero[30] who became a Jew against the wishes of the emperor.[31] His preeminence in Torah and logic was unquestioned, though the rabbis did not necessarily always follow his halachic opinions. His own scholarly superiority and genius were paradoxically his own undoing, for his colleagues could not really always understand the depth of his position and reasoning in halachic matters.[32]

He was a scribe by profession[33] and Rabi Yishmael told him: "Be careful, my son, for your work [as a scribe] is the work of heaven!"[34] To Rabi Meir, whatever he was doing was "the work of heaven." As mentioned above, he lived a very turbulent life. An assertive and controversial figure, he engaged in major struggles with his colleagues, and his viewpoint was almost always unacceptable to the majority. Despite the fact that in his own personal life and behavior he always followed the majority opinion—even when he disagreed with it![35]—his refusal to publicly accept the majority opinion on halachic matters led to an attempt by the rabbis to place a *cherem* (ban/ostracism) on him.[36] Though reminiscent of the story of Rabi

Eliezer ben Hyrkanos two generations earlier, unlike Rabi Eliezer, Rabi Meir successfully fought the ban.[37]

But he was always on the edge of controversy and even *cherem* (ostracism) due to his fiery independence, superior genius and confident nature. Rabi Meir felt that his strength of character and boldness of thought were positive attributes. He stated that these attributes are what earned for the Jewish people the gift of the Torah.[38] Regardless of the difficulties that these traits caused him during his life and career, he never changed them.

Rabi Meir was married to Bruriah, the eldest daughter of Rabi Chananya ben Tradyon.[39] Hers was a family destined to suffer enormous tragedies: Her father was one of the famous martyrs of Israel, wrapped in a Torah scroll and burned alive,[40] and her mother was also executed by the Romans at the same time. Her brother departed from his Jewish heritage—*yatza l'tarbus raah*—and was later slain by brigands.[41] Her younger sister was taken by the Romans and placed in a house of prostitution. She was delivered from that fate by the intervention of Rabi Meir—and the supernatural powers that he invoked—to save her, as well as the Roman jailer who aided the escape.[42] The famous Jewish incantation "God of Meir, answer me!" derives from this story of the rescue of Bruriah's sister.

Rabi Meir was forced to flee from the Land of Israel and Roman persecution because of this event.[43] We find Rabi Meir thereafter always on the move, rarely being able to find rest and security in any location. His master, Rabi Akiva, already saw him early in his life as perishing in a sea of travails.[44] But Rabi Meir somehow survived and flourished, riding the waves of life that passed him from the crest of one wave to the next and eventually depositing him safely on dry land.[45] Rabi Meir's life was always one of stormy seas and enormous waves. But he rode them into holiness, eternity and infinity.

Bruriah was one of the outstanding women of all time. She is quoted a number of times in the Talmud because of her wisdom and insights.[46] She was of a feisty nature and did not hold back from criticizing scholars, even colleagues of her husband, on Torah matters.[47] She was reputed to study hundreds of Torah lessons daily[48]

> "Behave very humbly before all human beings."
> *Rabi Meir*

and she was highly commended by the rabbis for explaining matters pertaining to the purity of vessels "better than did her father."[49] She was a woman of great physical attractiveness too.[50] Yet she and Rabi Meir knew great sadness, tension and tragedy in their married life together. Their two sons died on a Sabbath day, unbeknownst to Rabi Meir who was teaching Torah in the synagogue at the time. When he returned home, Bruriah gently informed him of their loss and comforted him, thereby helping him accept God's will. The story of this event is one of the most touching, heartbreaking and yet oddly comforting descriptions of the human condition in all of rabbinic literature.[51]

In a totally different and incomprehensible story related by Rashi, Rabi Meir once wished to prove to Bruriah that women were subject to lightheadedness and blandishments, and he therefore allowed one of his students to attempt to seduce her. As a result of this bizarre incident, Bruriah committed suicide out of despair and Rabi Meir fled from the Land of Israel out of intense shame.[52] There is an alternate theory to this tale, found in the tradition of Rabeinu Nissim (Gaon) ben Yaakov of Kairouan, Morocco. He relates that both Rabi Meir and Bruriah left together from the Land of Israel and journeyed to Babylonia to escape Roman persecution.[53] He makes no mention of the story later related by Rashi.

In either case, it seems clear that Rabi Meir never returned to the Land of Israel after his flight from the Romans. He died in Asia Minor (probably in what is today's Turkey) and asked to be buried near the sea so that the waters of the Mediterranean that had washed the shores of the Land of Israel would touch his bones as well, thus connecting him to his beloved homeland.[54] (So it is unlikely that the tomb of Rabi Meir Baal Haness in Tiberias is the grave of our Rabi Meir, all legend to the contrary notwithstanding.[55])

As mentioned above, the probable reason for Rabi Meir's flight was that he was a wanted fugitive from the Romans, due to his part in the rescue of his sister-in-law from degradation at their hands.[56] And yet another reason advanced for his departure from the Land of Israel (and from his students) was an aborted revolution that he and Rabi Nosson attempted against the authority of Raban Shimon ben Gamliel II, *Nasi* of the Sanhedrin. The Talmud relates that the students of the yeshivah and the general public had been accustomed to treat Rabi Meir, Rabi Nosson and Raban Shimon ben Gamliel II with equal displays of respect.[57] Raban Shimon ben Gamliel II, the son of Raban Gamliel II of Yavneh, followed his father's policy of strengthening the position and prestige of the *Nasi*, even at the expense of the honor of the other rabbis. Without any personal motives on his part, he felt that the office of the *Nasi* demanded the greatest respect. He insisted that the public no longer rise in honor of Rabi Meir and Rabi Nosson, as they had previously been wont to do, and that such public respect be shown exclusively to the *Nasi*. When Rabi Meir and Rabi Nosson entered the study hall on the following day, the assemblage—following Raban Shimon ben Gamliel II's instructions—did not rise in their honor. The two scholars felt that this method of strengthening the position of the *Nasi* was faulty, since it carried with it the possibility of causing public disrespect toward the other great Torah scholars.

To force the hand of Raban Shimon ben Gamliel II to adopt a different plan to raise the stature of the *Nasi*—and to exhibit to him how greatness in Torah should prevail even over official office—they decided to publicly discuss in the study hall those matters of *halachah*[58] in which Raban Shimon ben Gamliel II was yet deemed deficient in knowledge. They even planned to depose him eventually from his position of power and to appoint Rabi Meir as the new head of the court with Rabi Nosson as *Nasi*. Their intentions were in no way to obtain personal gain, but rather to clearly and publicly establish the supremacy of Torah scholarship in determining Jewish leadership. These two great scholars, in tandem, would then lead the Sanhedrin and its yeshivah.[59]

Raban Shimon ben Gamliel II got wind of their plans and prepared himself well for the halachic debate and successfully answered all questions posed to him by Rabi Meir and Rabi Nosson. To buttress further his policy on the supremacy of the position of the *Nasi* in Jewish life, he excluded Rabi Meir and Rabi Nosson from the study hall, citing their attempt to overthrow him and weaken his office as the reason. Rabi Meir and Rabi Nosson now remained outside the hall, nevertheless standing near a window and listening to the Torah discussions continuing inside. They continued to participate in the Torah debates of the Sanhedrin and its yeshivah through written notes that they threw through the window into the study hall. Love of Torah and of each other eventually overcame all of these policy decisions. Raban Shimon ben Gamliel II soon relented and granted them permission to return to the study hall due to their Torah prominence.

He punished them, however, for their attempted coup. Henceforth, their names would not be mentioned regarding any of their teachings. Rabi Nosson was now referred to by the euphemism *yesh omrim*—"there are those that say"; and Rabi Meir was now mentioned only as *acheirim*—"others say." In a dream, Rabi Nosson was told to apologize to Raban Shimon ben Gamliel II and he did so. Rabi Meir did not apologize: true to his nature of rational Torah interpretation, he retorted that dreams are of no real consequence.[60]

Because of all of these events and controversies, Rabi Meir became somewhat of a non-person in his own society. To a great extent, he thereafter assumed anonymity, even in the Mishnah. Rabi Yehudah HaNasi, the son of Raban Shimon ben Gamliel II, and the editor of the Mishnah, was ambivalent towards Rabi Meir. On one hand, he attributed his own phenomenal Torah achievements to the fact that he "glimpsed Rabi Meir from the back. I would have been even greater had I learned from him face to face!"[61] Yet, in many instances Rabi Yehudah HaNasi refused to attribute certain statements in *halachah* to Rabi Meir as their rightful author.[62] And in the Mishnah itself, the rule is "*stam mishnah Rabi Meir*"—i.e. an "anonymous *mishnah*" with no specified author, is that of Rabi Meir.[63] The Talmud metaphorically states that even God Himself, so to speak, initially refuses to quote Rabi Meir in the heavenly discussions of Torah.[64]

Rabi Meir became a lonely person, bereft of family and friends, and he left his beloved Land of Israel to wander in the exile of Asia Minor. It seems he was not overly concerned with his lot in life nor in the physical welfare of his descendants,[65] yet he was a tower of light for all later generations of the Jewish people. Even those who declared him to be "anonymous" remained his students and beneficiaries.

Uncompromising in his opinions and beliefs, he was never given to personal attacks. Yet even after Rabi Meir's death, Rabi Yehudah bar Eelai (his colleague throughout the pages of the Talmud) refused to allow the disciples of "anonymous" into his yeshivah, even when they petitioned to attend his lectures.[66] He correctly suspected that Rabi Meir's assertive nature and rugged independence had been transmitted to his students as well.

Nevertheless, it is obvious that without Rabi Meir and his great erudition and perseverance, the Mishnah that Rabi Yehudah HaNasi produced would not have been possible. Rabi Yehudah HaNasi built muscle and skin onto the skeleton of the Mishnah previously formulated by Rabi Meir.

Rabi Meir also is famous in the Talmud because of his relationship with *Acher,* Rabi Elishah ben Avuyah. A gifted scholar who became an apostate, Elishah lost his faith and became "another person." He was one of the primary teachers of Rabi Meir. The circumstances regarding Elishah's loss of faith—the disillusion he felt seeing Jews killed even while performing commandments, and the wanton executions by the Romans of the great scholars of Israel—are discussed in the Talmud.[67] He is also alleged to have entered the *Pardes*—the kabbalistic "orchard" of mystic supernaturalism and heavenly discovery. Apparently, that intense experience also shook his faith.[68] The Talmud also records that Elishah's father had impure motives in teaching him Torah—primarily wanting him to become recognized as a great scholar—and that this insincerity of purpose at the core of Elishah's education eventually affected him negatively.[69]

Because of these circumstances in his life, Elishah eventually chose to leave the faith of Judaism. There is an opinion that he even became a turncoat, helping the Romans in their persecution of the Jewish scholars. He encouraged the students of Torah to leave their study benches, seduced them with "Greek song" and preached blasphemy against Torah and tradition.[70] In spite of all of this, Rabi Meir did not completely forsake him. Amazingly enough, they even continued their high level Torah discussions. Rabi Meir was unafraid of the influence Elishah might exert on him, claiming himself able "to eat the inner contents of the fruit, while casting away the peel."[71]

Rabi Meir attempted to bring *Acher* back to traditional belief and observance. The long spiritual and intellectual struggles between the two—and *Acher's* desperate insistence that the Lord would not accept his repentance—is faithfully recorded for us in the Talmud.[72] Rabi Meir prays that *Acher* will be punished in the next world, so that after his punishment he will be allowed to somehow enter the blissful World to Come. Rabi Yochanan, two generations after the event, criticized Rabi Meir for this attitude. "Is it a courageous thing to [pray to] burn your mentor?" he asked. Because of his opinion in regard to *Acher*, upon Rabi Yochanan's death and ascent to the World to Come, *Acher's* punishment was remitted, and the fire emanating from his grave was finally extinguished.[73] There is a traditional opinion that one of the reasons that Rabi Meir was called *acheirim* was because of his continued relationship with *Acher*.[74] In any event, Rabi Meir is forever bound together with his tragic and spiritually lost mentor, Elishah ben Avuyah.

The ambivalence of Jewish history toward Elishah ben Avuyah to this day remains unresolved.[75] The rabbis quoted him in the Mishnah[76] and the Talmud[77] and did not erase his name from the annals of Jewish record. In a later generation, the great Rabi Yehudah HaNasi's bench was singed by a heavenly fire because he spoke ill of *Acher*.[78] After all, he had been a scholar so formidable that he was the mentor of Rabi Meir, and Rabi Meir's influence is felt throughout the pages of the Mishnah and the Talmud. In Jewish life, a child can save a parent, and a student can save a teacher from the oblivion of being forgotten.

Rabi Meir's sayings are scattered over all of the pages of the Talmud. Here is a short sampling of his wisdom:

- *He stated that wealth is good only if it brings serenity of spirit to its owner.*[79]
- *He strongly advised against allowing one's daughter to marry someone ignorant of Torah and boorish in behavior.*[80]

- *One should train one's son in a profession that is "clean and light" and teach him to pray to God for his sustenance and success.*[81]

- *If slander succeeds and survives, it must contain an element of truth within it.*[82]

- *Look not at the container, but rather at its contents.*[83]

- *One enters the world with clenched fists—ready to grab everything—and one departs the world with open hands, having taken nothing with him.*[84]

- *Happy is one who was raised in Torah and toiled in its study and support, and brought satisfaction to one's Creator, and grew to have a good name, and left this world having a good name.*[85]

In the *sefer Torah* of Rabi Meir, it was written that the garments that God fashioned for Adam and Chava were made from light.[86] Rabi Meir himself was fashioned from light.

Rabi Meir had great love for the Jewish people and the Land of Israel. As we see from his experiences with *Acher*, he also had abounding tolerance for Jewish sinners.[87] He remembered all of his life the words of Bruriah that one should pray that sin should disappear from the face of the earth, but not that the sinners themselves should be destroyed.[88] He debated with the Roman authorities and explained Judaism to them.[89] As could be expected, he defended and complimented non-Jews who became converts to Judaism,[90] and even criticized those who unnecessarily delayed their conversion to Judaism.[91]

Rabi Meir's formula for entry into the World to Come is a relatively simple one: "Anyone who dwells in the Land of Israel, proclaims the *Shma* (the prayer that affirms the beliefs of Jewish monotheism and God's unity) morning and evening, and speaks Hebrew, the holy tongue, is destined to be in the World to Come."[92] It was he who said that Moshe wrote the last verses of the Torah regarding his own death not with ink, but with his very own tears.[93] And the same can be said of Rabi Meir himself: he wrote his life's story in his own tears. He taught that the great Torah scholars of Israel should be mourned in no less a manner than the King of Israel[94]

"Look not at the container but rather at its contents."
Rabi Meir

THE ORAL LAW OF SINAI

and indeed, Rabi Meir is mourned, remembered and treasured by all of Israel for all time.

Among the main scholars who were contemporaries and colleagues of Rabi Meir were Rabi Yehudah ben Eelai,[95] Rabi Yosi ben Chalafta,[96] Rabi Shimon bar Yochai,[97] Rabi Elazar ben Shamua,[98] Rabi Yochanan HaSandlar, Rabi Nosson (HaBavli), Rabi Yehoshua ben Korcha,[99] Rabi Yaakov ben Korshai,[100] Rabi Eliezer, the son of Rabi Yosi HaGlili and Raban Shimon ben Gamliel II, the *Nasi*. Rabi Yehoshua ben Levi lived a long life and was also active at the time of Rabi Meir.[101]

Tomb of Rabi Yochanan HaSandlar, Mount Meron

Raban Shimon ben Gamliel II

After the incident with Rabi Meir and Rabi Nosson, Raban Shimon ben Gamliel II consolidated his leadership position. He had great halachic authority; in the Talmud, the law always remained as his declared opinion, with only three exceptions.[102] His decisions were considered clear and final.[103] In spite of his strong and open policy of strengthening the power and prestige of the *Nasi,* he was personally a man of great humility.[104] Perhaps it was precisely because of his tendency to be pliant and humble that he was forced to take strong measures to punish Rabi Meir and Rabi Nosson for their attempted coup; he saw his task as safeguarding the authority of the position of *Nasi.*

What else do we know of him? Very little about his personal life. However, Raban Shimon's words of wisdom and Torah law are found everywhere in the Talmud and his prestige was great among the people of Israel. According to Talmudic sources, he warned against unnecessarily arguing with the great scholars, for "Wherever the scholars affixed their eyes, either death or poverty followed."[105] He was aware of human foibles and of the politics involved in leading the people and the yeshivah.[106] He postulated the rule that the rabbis should never proclaim any decree that the majority of the Jewish community will find too difficult to abide by.[107] He also stated that a father had a right to disinherit children who did not behave properly.[108] He stated that those commandments

RABAN SHIMON BEN GAMLIEL II
c. 170 CE

Teachers
- Raban Gamliel II
- Rabi Tarfon

Student
- Rabi Yehudah HaNasi

Colleagues
- Rabi Meir
- Rabi Yehudah bar Eelai
- Rabi Shimon bar Yochai
- Rabi Elazar ben Shimon
- Rabi Eliezer ben Rabi Yosi HaGlili

Relatives
- Father: Raban Gamliel II
- Son: Rabi Yehudah HaNasi

that the Jewish people accepted on themselves with joy and enthusiasm remain solid within the people for all times,[109] and that all Jews are royalty.[110]

Marcus Aurelius ascended the throne of Rome in 161 CE. Some time after the beginning of his reign, Raban Shimon ben Gamliel II passed away. The death of Raban Shimon was a tragic event for the Jews in the Land of Israel, not only because an outstanding leader had died but primarily because bitter events followed hard on his demise. During his lifetime, his *zechus* (merit) had protected the Jewish people, and even the crops from natural disasters. After his death, a plague of locusts descended on the country, ruining the crops and orchards,[111] and the local Roman authorities reimposed decrees on the Jewish population that again restricted their rights to observe the tenets of Judaism.[112]

The beginning of the reign of Marcus Aurelius was marked by social turbulence and imperial wars. The Parthian Empire, the ancient enemy of Rome, tested the new emperor, whom they knew to be more philosopher than warrior. When they attacked the Romans in Babylonia and Syria, the war drew perilously close to the Land of Israel. Much of the local population in the area that had previously been pacified by the Romans now rose against them. Marcus Aurelius counterattacked and drove the Parthians back, deep into Afghanistan, and even as far as Armenia. In the process, he crushed hopes for an incipient Jewish revolt as well.

Marcus Aurelius, circa 160-180 CE

Remembering the nearly successful Jewish rebellion of Bar Kochba 25 years earlier, the local Roman authorities in the Land of Israel moved to further prevent the Jews from using the Roman preoccupation with these new wars to rise against them again. They felt that the best means to do this was restricting the observance of Judaism, for Rome recognized that the Jewish national spirit of Israel was fueled by its loyalty to Torah and its observance of Torah commandments. The Jews made loud and massive demonstrations against this new persecution, confident that the tolerant and understanding emperor would sympathize with their cause. They were correct in this assessment, as the decrees were rescinded by Marcus Aurelius simultaneously with the conclusion of the Parthian war.

Now, for perhaps the first time in two centuries, peace and quiet rested upon the Jewish community in the Land of Israel. The almost 20-year reign[113] of Marcus Aurelius afforded an unusual opportunity for the revival of Jewish life and Torah scholarship in the Land of Israel.

> "Wherever the scholars affixed their eyes [in disapproval] either death or poverty followed."
> *Raban Shimon Ben Gamliel II*

Rabi Yehudah HaNasi

RABI YEHUDAH HANASI
c. 185 CE
Teachers
- Raban Shimon ben Gamliel II
- Rabi Tarfon
- Rabi Nosson

Students
- Rabi Levi ben Sissas
- Rabi Shimon ben Rabi
- Raban Gamliel III
- Rabi Chiya
- Yehudah ben Rabi Chiya
- Chezkiah ben Rabi Chiya
- Rav (Abba bar Ayvu)
- Mar Shmuel
- Rav Abba bar Abba
- Rabi Shimon ben Elazar
- Rav Chanina bar Choma
- Rabi Oshiya
- Rabi Yanai
- Rabi Yochanan
- Rabi Shimon ben Lakish

Colleagues
- Sumchos
- Bar Kapara
- Rabi Elazar ben Shimon
- Rabi Yishmael ben Rabi Yosi ben Chalafta
- Rabi Menachem ben Rabi Yosi ben Chalafta
- Rabi Yosi ben Rabi Yehudah bar Eelai
- Rabi Shimon ben Yehudah of Acco
- Rabi Eliezer ben Yehudah of Eevilim
- Rabi Chiya
- Rabi Yitzchak ben Avdimi

Relatives
- Father: Raban Shimon ben Gamliel II
- Sons: Raban Gamliel III, Rabi Shimon ben Rabi

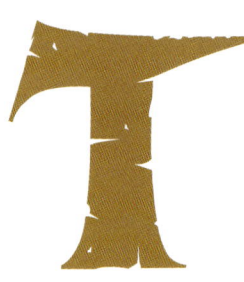

This period in history coincided with the rise of one of the all-time main pillars of Jewish life, Rabi Yehudah HaNasi, to the position of *Nasi*. The son of Raban Shimon ben Gamliel II, Rabi Yehudah's preeminence in Torah was so well recognized by his colleagues and the Jewish people at large that he came to be called simply Rabi, "my teacher and master."[114] He was also known as *Rabeinu HaKadosh*—"our holy master and teacher." This title was earned by his intense piety and holy behavior.[115] It would be Rabi who would gather all of the scholars of Israel at his places of residence[116] and together with them fashion the Mishnah in its final form as we know it today.[117] This accomplishment is in distinct contrast to the previous few generations when scholars operated their own individual schools of Torah learning throughout the country and could not meet together regularly and continually to clarify matters of *halachah* and Torah interpretation.

Now that the benign Marcus Aurelius was emperor, and the decrees against Torah and its scholars were abolished, Rabi was able to reestablish the halcyon days of Rabi Yochanan ben Zakai's Yavneh, albeit in a different location. Rabi stated that the troubles that befell Israel were caused directly by ignorance and neglect of Torah study.[118] The dramatic change in atmosphere between the Roman governors and the Jews living in the Land of Israel stemmed directly from the personal friendship between Rabi and the Roman emperor, called in the Talmud by the name of Antoninus.[119]

When and how this amity developed is not clear. Most scholars think that it occurred when Marcus Aurelius came east during the Parthian war.[120] It is also possible that Marcus Aurelius visited the Land of Israel before becoming emperor and Rabi came to meet him. There are numerous legends regarding the beginnings of their comradeship, even that they were exchanged at birth to save Rabi's life![121] Legendary figures and events always inspire new legends of their own.

In any event, the personal bond between the two leaders enabled Rabi to undertake his monumental project of completing and disseminating the Mishnah.[122] Rabi and Antoninus are described as being the prime descendants of Yaakov and Eisav[123] and a paradigm of what the relationship between the brothers could have been. In fact, Antoninus is reputed to have presented a candelabra to a synagogue and received Rabi's blessing for so doing.[124] There is even an opinion that Antoninus secretly converted to Judaism,[125] though there is an explicit contrary opinion as well.[126] Whether or not this conversion took place, Rabi guaranteed Antoninus entry into the World to Come.[127]

Rabi and Antoninus discussed all aspects of human life and the world about them. Their discussions and conversations are recorded in many places in the Talmud and throughout rabbinic literature.[128] Moreover, Rabi is reported to have given Antoninus advice on how to handle his enemies in Rome and how to arrange for the succession of his son to the imperial throne.[129] Though Antoninus provided Rabi with an honor guard to protect him from malcontents,[130] Rabi relied on his own prayers to protect him from untoward incidents and personages.[131] Antinonus died first, and Rabi deeply mourned his death, stating that "the bundle [the personal attachment between Rome and the Jews] is now parted and severed."[132]

One of the things that had cemented their friendship, in addition to their rich intellects, was that Rabi and Antoninus were both fabulously wealthy. As proof of this, the Talmud tells us that each had the luxury of fresh vegetables on his table year-round.[133] At one

> "I have not benefited from the pleasures of this world not even a small finger's worth."
>
> *Rabi Yehudah HaNasi*

point, Rabi refused to accept bags of gold sent to him by Antoninus, protesting that his riches were more than adequate to sustain him.[134] From the time of Moshe onwards, we do not find greatness in Torah knowledge and behavior coupled with enormous prosperity such as Rabi's:[135] it was of such magnitude that even his stable masters were wealthier than kings of local tribes.[136] His own fabulous wealth was estimated to be greater than that of King David and King Shlomo.[137]

Yet Rabi's fortune caused him problems with other scholars. The Talmud relates that the holy man, Rabi Pinchas ben Yair (about whom it was said that even his donkey was able to distinguish between fodder that had been tithed and fodder that had not been tithed[138]) refused to enter Rabi's house because of the rare, expensive, dangerous and powerful donkeys that were in Rabi's stables. Rabi Pinchas felt that Rabi should not keep such dangerous animals on his premises,[139] even if he could afford them easily.

The Mishnah in Avos [140] states that there are seven qualities that are fitting for the righteous. One of those seven[141] is great prosperity. Rabi and his sons possessed all of the qualities mentioned there.[142] But enormous wealth by itself, without the taming influences of wisdom, piety, maturity and public social responsibility, can destroy its owner. Perhaps that is why the rabbis emphasized that Rabi embodied *all* of the seven qualities—for having the quality of affluence alone is no guarantee of righteousness. However, in the hands of a person such as Rabi—"Our Holy Teacher/*Rabeinu HaKadosh*"—it became an important tool for good, and the basis for the accomplishment of significant and lasting projects. Rabi's legendary wealth certainly gave him the influence and the means to develop, edit and publish the Mishnah. That is another reason why the rabbis of the Talmud so warmly endorsed his stature, and saw his phenomenal means as a positive spiritual asset.

Rabi clearly regarded his abundant funds as an important tool to support the needy and feed the hungry,[143] and therefore he had great respect for wealth for its potential uses and for those who distributed their riches wisely.[144] And Rabi practiced what he preached, opening his granaries to all in years of drought and economic privation.¹⁴⁵ His generosity and kindheartedness were common knowledge throughout the Jewish world. Rabi could not withhold his tears of mercy even for the descendants of enemies, and granted them financial support.¹⁴⁶

Because of this well-earned reputation, Rabi was held to high standards of behavior. In Heaven, the righteous—those who are nearest to God, so to speak—are judged exactingly, even by "a hair's breadth."¹⁴⁷ When he sent a frightened calf that was hiding under his cloak to slaughter—admonishing it that this was its function in the world—he was severely punished with painful urinary problems.¹⁴⁸ Yet Rabi preached that pain and tribulations in life are to be desired and held dear, for they serve to cleanse a person of sin and hubris.¹⁴⁹ Rabi also suffered greatly from dental problems for thirteen years, until he was cured by the prophet Eliyahu who appeared to him in the form of his student, Rabi Chiya.¹⁵⁰ Though we may not fathom the Heavenly ledger, according to the Talmud, Rabi's suffering and holiness protected the Jewish people, so that no woman died in childbirth or miscarried during the thirteen years of Rabi's agonizing illnesses.¹⁵¹

Tomb of Rabi Yehudah HaNasi, Tzippori

In fact, despite Rabi's wealth, piety and prominence, he had much physical suffering in his lifetime due to his very delicate physical constitution.¹⁵² Because of his continual concerns over the physical and spiritual state of the Jewish people, as well his own personal pains and suffering, Rabi was always in a serious mood.¹⁵³ His disciple, Rav Levi ben Sissas, attempted to bring cheer into Rabi's life, if even for a moment,¹⁵⁴ but the Talmud reports that were Rabi to relax his serious mien, troubles upon Israel would automatically follow.¹⁵⁵

On his deathbed, Rabi raised his ten fingers heavenward and proclaimed: "O, Creator of the Universe, You know that I have used my hands exclusively to labor in your Torah, and I have not benefited in pleasure from this world even a small finger's worth!"¹⁵⁶

THE ORAL LAW OF SINAI

meaning that never had he been carried away by his wealth nor indulged in extravagance for his own enjoyment.

As we review his life, we see that Rabi was forgiving in his nature and loyal to his colleagues and disciples. Aware that they had strayed from Torah observance, he searched out the descendants of his colleague, Rabi Elazar ben Shimon, and that of his mentor, Rabi Tarfon, in order to restore them to the proper path of Jewish life.[157] When, as a youth, he compared himself to Rabi Elazar ben Shimon in Torah knowledge and holiness, Rabi felt humbled, for his own father had informed him that Rabi Elazar was entitled to greater honor, "for he is a lion, the son of a lion (Rabi Shimon bar Yochai), while you are only a lion, the son of a fox."[158] Apparently this opinion was shared by the widow of Rabi Elazar, who rebuffed Rabi's proposal to marry her with the rhetorical question: "A vessel that served in holiness should now be asked to serve the mundane?"[159]

Stone carving of a menorah in a burial cave, Beis Shearim

Furthermore, Rabi was quick to retract his opinion in favor of others' opinions when he saw that their position had merit.[160] The prophet Eliyahu was a frequent guest in Rabi's yeshivah,[161] and the students there were people of great powers and immense scholarship. Among them were Rabi Chiya and his sons[162] whom Rabi praised for disseminating Torah, declaring his accomplishments to be immense.[163] Rabi Chiya, in turn, attributed all of his achievements to the teachings and influence of Rabi.[164]

Though Rabi's modesty and personal humility were legendary,[165] like his father and grandfather before him he was zealous in preserving the honor of the office of *Nasi*.[166] There is a delicate line between maintaining personal humility and preserving the honor of the public position that one occupies. Rabi managed to balance successfully on that line.

One of the leading disciples of Rabi was Rabi Levi ben Sissas.[167] Rabi thought very highly of him, considering him to be his equal. He recommended him for a leading rabbinic position and stood by him in his difficulties in maintaining that position.[168] Among Rabi's colleagues were Sumchos, the student of Rabi Meir; Bar Kapara;[169] Rabi Elazar ben Shimon; the son of Rabi Shimon bar Yochai and his son, Rabi Shimon ben Elazar; the sons of Rabi Yosi ben Chalafta—especially Yishmael and Menachem; Rabi Yosi ben Yehudah, the son of Rabi Yehudah ben Eelai; Rabi Shimon ben Yehudah of Acco, a disciple of Rabi Shimon bar Yochai as well; and Rabi Eliezer (Elazar) ben Yehudah of Eevlim, in the Galilee. Among his most famous students were his own sons, Rabi Shimon and Raban Gamliel III; Rav Abba (Aricha) bar Ayvu, known simply as Rav; Mar Shmuel; Rabi Chiya[170] and his sons, Yehudah and Chezkiah; Rav Chanina bar Chama; Abba bar Abba;[171] Rabi Oshiya;[172] Rabi Yanai;[173] Rabi Yochanan[174] and his brother-in-law, Rav Shimon ben (Reish) Lakish.[175]

Rabi Chiya

RABI CHIYA
175-205 CE

Teacher
- Rabi Yehudah HaNasi

Colleagues
- Rabi Yitzchak ben Avdimi
- Rabi Yehudah HaNasi
- Rabi Yosi ben Rabi Yehudah bar Eelai
- Rabi Levi ben Sissas

Students
- Rav (Abba bar Ayvu)
- Yehudah bar Rabi Chiya
- Chezkiyah bar Rabi Chiya
- Zeirei I

Relatives
- Sons: Chezkiyah ben Rabi Chiya, Yehudah ben Rabi Chiya
- Nephew: Rav (Abba bar Ayvu)

Rabi Chiya has the distinction of being regarded as both a disciple and colleague of Rabi. The Talmud asserts that if "Rabi did not teach [this law] then how would Rav Chiya known of it?"[176] Rabi Chiya is seen as the leader of the transition generation between the men of the Mishnah—the *Tannaim*—and the scholars of the Talmud—the *Amoraim*. He was also active in facilitating the movement of the main Torah center from the Land of Israel to Babylonia after the death of Rabi. Because Rabi had taught him the different ways of interpreting *halachah,* Rabi Chiya stated that "Rabi gave me life!"[177] Rabi Chiya was a man of wealth: a flax dealer.[178] Scrupulously honest in his business behavior, he went past the letter of the law in his dealings with others;[179] and because of his dedication to Torah study and piety, the flax crop never failed in the Land of Israel, nor did wine spoil in the casks while he and his sons lived there.[180] The prophet Eliyahu compared Rabi Chiya and his sons to the *Avos*—the forefathers of the Jewish people.[181]

Rabi Chiya's Torah lectures were compared to fire itself.[182] While living in the Land of Israel, he based himself in Tiberias,[183] the center of the linen and silk trade. Yet, his entire life and mindset were focused on Torah study—so much so, that Rabi sent two guards to always accompany Rabi Chiya while he walked, so that in his constant concentration on Torah he should not injure himself.[184] As one who came from Babylonia to the Land of Israel, Rabi Chiya was unable to pronounce the letter *ches* in the same accent of those living in Israel, and was chided for this failure by Rabi![185] But the prophet Eliyahu himself interceded on behalf of Rabi Chiya, to insist that Rabi should always honor him.[186]

Rabi Chiya died in the Land of Israel and was buried in the vicinity of Tiberias, but the exact location of his burial cave was not known, even in the generation that immediately succeeded him.[187] This anonymity was seen as a reward and a merit for Rabi Chiya, who had traveled widely to spread Torah study to the Jewish people.[188] All of his life, he had illuminated Jews far and wide about the rewards for satiating one's self with Torah knowledge.[189]

His teachings were unique: the Talmud tells us that Rabi Chiya had a "hidden" scroll containing traditions and halachic decisions from previous generations.[190] He preached that silence is a great and positive virtue.[191] Like Rabi, he respected the wealthy and honored the charitable.[192] A source of comfort to his people, Rabi Chiya taught that God would never completely forsake Israel, even in the worst of moments and trials.[193]

If it can be said that Rabi Chiya's Torah greatness was a result of his being a disciple of Rabi, it is no exaggeration to say that Rabi's lifework of the Mishnah survived and prospered because of the effort and teachings of Rabi Chiya. Rabi himself exclaimed: "How great are the deeds and accomplishments of Chiya!"[194] And so they are.

The sons of Rabi Chiya were Chezkiyah and Yehudah. They were regarded as "twins," though the Talmud tells us that they were actually born some time apart.[195] They are seen as still belonging to the generations of *Tannaim*—the people of the Mishnah,[196] though in effect they serve as a transition generation to the time of the *Amoraim*—the men of the Talmud. In this respect, they are in the same category as Rav, who is considered to have the lofty authority of a *Tanna*,[197] though his main work was during the first generation of *Amoraim*.

The brothers worked in agriculture,[198] though naturally their fame and reputation were derived through their labor in studying and teaching Torah. Their concentration and focus on learning

> **"How great are the actions of Chiya [in restoring Torah to Israel]."**
> *Talmud Bavli, Bava Metzia*

Torah intently caused considerable wonderment.[199] Like his father, Chezkiyah promoted the supreme value of peace,[200] and his main base of study and influence was Tiberias.[201] After the death of Rabi, the cities of Tzipori[202] and Beis Shearim[203] in the lower Galilee declined as Torah centers, and Tiberias became the main city of Jewish learning and commercial life in the Land of Israel. Chezkiyah is quoted many times in the Talmud, yet his brother, Yehudah, is hardly mentioned by name at all as authoring halachic opinions. It may very well be that Yehudah's opinions and teachings are subsumed in the recorded opinions of his "twin." Whether quoted directly or not, these two sons of Rabi Chiya are together raised to the pedestal of holiness and scholarship throughout the pages of the Talmud.

Wine pressing surface, Ashtamoa (near Hevron), late Roman/Byzantine period

The Writing of the Mishnah

The period of tranquility between Rome and the Jews that was the norm during the reign of Marcus Aurelius was continued after his death in 180 CE during the reign of Commodus, his son and successor as the emperor of Rome. However, the warmth of personal friendship that existed between Rabi and Marcus Aurelius was no longer present. Rabi sensed that the window of opportunity for Jewish spiritual autonomy and Torah development that existed during his friendship with Marcus Aurelius would soon shut. To guard against the likely loss of the *mesorah* of Torah teachings, he made the fateful decision to gather all of the traditions of the Oral Law together in book form—the Mishnah.

This bold innovation required considerable justification because it was apparently in violation of the precept that "the words of the Oral Law are not to be committed [in a permanent and public fashion] to writing."[204] Rabi wrote the Mishnah as a public book of study in order to save the Torah, using the exception to the rule provided by the verse in Psalms (119:126) "There is a time to do for God, they have annulled Your Torah," for he read that verse to mean: "There is a time to do for God, even if it appears to violate Your Torah's rules."[205] This interpretation of the verse is very delicate and therefore rarely used. One cannot easily violate a Torah rule in order to accomplish what one thinks to be an act for God. Tragically, in the history of the Jewish people many groups and

> "There is a time to do for God."
> *Psalms 119:126*

individuals, misusing and misreading the importance of this rule, eventually have fallen away from Torah observance and even from Jewish identity. Only someone of the stature, erudition and pious holiness of Rabi could make this radical move and convince the scholars of Israel to join him.

The circumstances mandating their valiant action are described to us by the two later pillars of Judaism, Rashi (Rabbi Shlomo ben Yitzchak of eleventh century France) and Rambam (Rabbi Moshe ben Maimon of twelfth century Spain, Morocco and Egypt). Rashi writes:

> *Since from the time of the disciples of Shammai and Hillel, three generations before him [meaning Rabi], there were great disputes regarding the meanings of the Torah and there arose the possibility of there being two Torahs amongst Israel, due to the oppression of the kingdom [Rome] and the evil decrees passed against Israel. Because of these [troubles] they [the scholars of Israel] were unable to clarify the differing opinions and settle them, until [came] the time of Rabi. Then did the Lord give favor unto Rabi in the eyes of the Roman emperor, Antoninus, and the troubles subsided and Rabi was able to gather all of the scholars of the Land of Israel to him [in Beis Shearim and Tzipori]. Until his [Rabi's] days there were no ordered tractates [of the Oral Law] but rather every student studied and reviewed lectures that he heard from the great men and he ascribed to them these teachings—"this halachah I heard from this and this scholar." Now, when they all gathered together [at Rabi's yeshivah], each of the scholars repeated what he had learned and together they worked to clarify the reasons behind disparate opinions and they settled as to which opinion was to be deemed correct. And then they ordered these opinions and decisions into tractates: the laws of torts by themselves, the laws of levirate marriages by themselves, the laws of the Temple service by themselves, [etc.]. And they quoted the opinions and decisions of many scholars anonymously, for Rabi agreed with their decisions and therefore quoted them anonymously in order to indicate that so is the halachah.*[206]

In the introduction to his monumental work, *Mishneh Torah*, Rambam writes:

> *Rabeinu HaKadosh [Our holy teacher, Rabi] compiled the Mishnah. From the days of Moshe Rabeinu there was never a book that gathered the laws of the Oral Law that was taught publicly. Rather, in each and every generation the head of the Beis Din [Sanhedrin] or the prophet that lived in that generation wrote down for himself the lectures in Torah that were delivered by the scholars and then he [the head of the Beis Din and/or prophet] taught these matters publicly and orally. And so it was that each of the scholars wrote for his own use a work that according to his ability explained the laws and Torah that he had learned from his teachers. And the teachings that were renewed in every generation and the laws that were derived through the use of the Thirteen Principles [of the Oral Law that are used to interpret the Written Law] and were approved by the Sanhedrin [were also recorded in notebooks]. And so did this procedure continue until the time of Rabeinu HaKadosh and he gathered all of the teachings, laws, explanations, interpretations, and traditions that were learned from Moshe Rabeinu and from the Sanhedrin of each generation thereafter, and he organized it all and wrote everything in a book, the Mishnah. And this book was taught publicly to all of Israel and everyone made copies of it and it was disseminated everywhere. This was so that the Torah of the Oral Law would not be forgotten from Israel. And why did Rabeinu HaKadosh do so then? Why did he not leave matters the same as they had been until then? Because he saw that the Torah students were decreasing in number, that the troubles and oppressions facing Israel were being renewed and increasing, that the Roman Empire was becoming ever more powerful and expanding throughout the world, and that the Jewish people were scattering unto the ends of the earth. He therefore composed a written work that could be in the hands of all, so that all Jews could study [the Oral Law] quickly and easily and so that it should not be forgotten. [Then] Rabi sat together with his Beis Din for the balance of his life and taught the Mishnah publicly to the multitudes.*[207]

Both Rashi and Rambam base their statements on the note that appears in the *Iggeres Rav Sherira Gaon* [208] which explains that, "In the days of Rabi, the Torah students were freed from all concerns of religious persecution and restrictions due to the personal friendship that existed between Rabi and Antoninus, and therefore all [the scholars] agreed then to establish the law [and halachic tradition in writing]."

Rabi was not a prophet, but he was blessed with Godly foresight. His father, Raban Shimon ben Gamliel II, had stated: "Who is the wise person? One who sees what events will yet be forthcoming."[209] Undoubtedly, he must have had his son in mind as being such a wise person, for Rabi foresaw the immediate and imperative need for a written, publicly disseminated Mishnah. This is yet another example of the truth of the words of the rabbis, "A wise person is even greater than a prophet."[210]

Yet many times, a person with vision does not possess the will or the courage to act upon his view of things to come. This was not the case with Rabi. He indeed was the wise person who preserved Torah and Israel with his astute foresight. We have seen earlier that in spite of his pliant and peaceful nature, he was firm in defending the honor of the position of *Nasi*. Now he took the courageous, unprecedented and apparently "illegal" act of permanently committing the Oral Law to writing for public use. It was the admiration, respect and love that all of his colleagues and all of Israel felt for him that allowed Rabi to propose, facilitate and eventually execute this new step. His action was also a demonstration of Rabi's belief that with one correct act performed at a fortuitous moment one may fulfill one's role in life and gain entry into the World to Come.[211] Rabi wept when he said this.[212]

The correctness of Rabi's position has been vindicated by all of the succeeding centuries of Jewish life and Torah scholarship. Where would we be without the Mishnah and its later child, the Talmud? Would there be a Jewish people at all today? The entire future of Jewish survival lay in the balance scale before Rabi. "Blessed be He that has chosen them [the Torah scholars of Israel] and their teachings [and decisions]."[213] Blessed be the Lord Who gave Rabi to the Jewish people.

The organization of the Mishnah by Rabi divided the Oral Law into six distinct sections: thus, the official title of the Mishnah is *Shishah Sidrei Mishnah*[214]—The Six Orders of Mishnah. These six orders are:

- *Zeraim* (agricultural laws and blessings)
- *Moed* (Sabbath and holy days)
- *Nashim* (marriage, divorce, vows)
- *Nezikin* (torts, damages, business laws, the judicial system)
- *Kodashim* (the Temple and its sacrifices and rituals)
- *Taharos* (laws of purity and impurity)

The Talmud attaches this organizational order of the Mishnah to a verse in Yeshayahu, 33:6.[215] The six individual *sedarim* are themselves further subdivided into tractates covering specific subject matter relating to the general category of that particular order.

The order of Zeraim is made up of eleven tractates;[216] Moed, twelve tractates;[217] Nashim, seven tractates;[218] Nezikin, ten tractates;[219] Kodashim, eleven tractates;[220] and Taharos, twelve tractates.[221] All in all, there are 63 tractates to the Mishnah.[222]

The order of the tractates within the larger order of the *seder* has been a subject of scholarly discussion in itself over the ages.

Opposite page: Detail of the mosaic floor depicting David playing the harp from the Gaza synagogue, circa 6th Century CE (Israel Museum, Jerusalem)

Rav Sherira Gaon (tenth century, Babylonia), in his famous historical work mentioned above, *Iggeres Rav Sherira Gaon,* wrote:

Regarding the order of the tractates, when Rabi wrote the Mishnah he did not place the particular tractates in any exact order, but they were edited individually and we do not know which tractates were [completed and edited] earlier or later… and therefore if one wishes to change the order of the tractates, he may do so. Nevertheless, we do see in the Talmud regarding certain tractates such as Sotah, Nazir, Makos, [and] Shevuos that there was an established order of the placement of the tractates…

Though it is not explicitly clear from his writings, Rav Sherira Gaon seems to say that there is no set order to the individual tractates appearing in a *seder,* unless the Talmud itself insists that there is a definite connection between the order and placement of certain tractates one after the other.[223]

However, Rambam in his introduction to his Commentary to the Mishnah, *Peirush HaMishnayos,* states that there is a definite reason and pattern to the order of the individual tractates within a *seder* of Mishnah; and furthermore that all inferences in the Talmud that there is no order to the tractates[224] merely refer to the fact that we are unaware of which tractate of the Mishnah Rabi completed and publicized first, but that in his final editing of the Mishnah there was a definite order of the tractates. Rambam then proceeds to give his reasoning for why the order of the tractates in every *seder* appears as it does.

Rabi Menachem HaMeiri (c. 1350) in his *Beis HaBechirah,* "Introduction to Tractate *Avos,*" follows the Rambam in ascribing order to the place of the appearance of tractates in every *seder* of Mishnah. However, his order of tractates and the reasoning therefore differs from that of Rambam. Over the ages, many scholars have attempted to explain the pattern and order of the tractates in Mishnah. One of the great later scholars of the previous generation, Rabi Reuven Margoliyus, proposed a novel, yet simple, explanation for the order of the tractates within a *seder* of the Mishnah. He states that the order was based upon the number of chapters in each tractate: the tractate having the most chapters within it came first, the tractate with the second most chapters within it was placed second, and so on down the line.[225] To every rule there are exceptions, and Rabbi Margoliyus satisfactorily (to my mind, at least) explains away the few apparent exceptions to this rule.[226] The names of the individual tractates were well known among the scholars of Israel, even before Rabi's formalizing them in the Mishnah.[227] In any event, the Mishnah—as we have it in our hands today—contains six *sedarim* and is comprised of 63 tractates, all now printed in the traditional order as they have appeared in manuscript and print over the last several centuries.

Rabi incorporated in the final edition of the Mishnah the private notebooks of the previous generations of the scholars of Israel.[228] Among them were *Mishnah Rishonah*—the original and first recordings of the teachings of the Oral Law from the time of the Men of the Great Assembly through the times of Hillel and Shammai.[229] The Talmud states: "*Mishnah Rishonah* was never removed from its place [in the Mishnah]."[230] Rabi also included the notebooks of the students of Rabi Akiva and Rabi Yishmael.[231] The voluminous notebook of Rabi Meir was then added and Rabi instituted the rule that *stam mishnah Rabi Meir*, i.e. a *mishnah* that contains no name of any scholar within its text is attributed to Rabi Meir and his notebook.[232] Rabi also included the Mishnah notebook of Rabi Nosson, who was one of his teachers and mentors.[233] Rabi Nosson apparently had been the last major contributor to the "database" of the Mishnah before Rabi's edition.

Rabi collected all of these works, then studied, edited and organized them.[234] Together with all of the halachic material and decisions of Rabi's own colleagues and yeshivah, and his own personal opinions, this vast compendium of knowledge and law became the Mishnah.[235] It was a monumental and complicated task: There were texts that had portions of them missing and thus were not really understandable. Nevertheless, Rabi copied those texts exactly as they were, leaving it to the later scholars of the Talmud to fill in the word gaps and provide the proper understanding of that Mishnah.[236] That process is the origin of the statement that appears so often in the Talmud: "*chisurei mechsara*"[237]—meaning that there are words missing in the text of this *mishnah* and the text should be emended in this fashion, as now explained in the Talmud, and that the Mishnah should be understood as correctly reading such and such. Rabi would not change the unusual wording of previous notebooks of the Mishnah,[238] even when the ultimate halachic decision of that notebook nonetheless would have been preserved in his Mishnah.[239]

Rabi's genius lay in the organization of such an enormous amount of material into manageable sections and paragraphs and in developing the beautiful and simple prose style of mishnaic Hebrew. This prose and language style became the norm for well over a millennia of later rabbinic writings, the foremost example of which is the *Mishneh Torah* of Rambam.[240] The Mishnah has a rhythm to it, a cadence and beat that helps the student along in studying and remembering it. Torah is compared to a song;[241] and Rabi is the unseen conductor of the music of the Mishnah.

Rabi was determined to teach Torah to the masses,[242] no matter what external conditions existed. No outside influences—no hint of the turbulent times that swirl about its composition—find expression in Rabi's work. The temporary, depressing and ever-changing world never is allowed to intrude into the eternal world outlined on the pages of Rabi's Mishnah. This great compendium of the Oral Law has its own distinctive melody and refrain which can be heard distinctively in the overall majestic music of Torah that echoes from Sinai.

Rabi was unable to gather all of the scholars in one place to decide definitively all of the matters discussed in the Mishnah. Because of this handicap, the Mishnah did not have the unquestioned authority of the decisions of the earlier Sanhedrins. Therefore, we find that in many instances the *Amoraim*, the latter scholars of the Talmud, differed with the express opinions and decisions of the Mishnah.[243] Nevertheless, the Mishnah remained the "iron pillar" of the Oral Law[244] and the basis for all halachic decisions in the Talmud. Therefore, the Talmud is essentially an exposition of the Mishnah, and is meant to provide a detailed understanding of its

Detail from the mosaic floor of the Sepphoris synagogue, circa 5th century CE

words, values and principles. It is the Mishnah that brings one to study and understand the intricacies of the Talmud.²⁴⁵

But the Mishnah did not exist alone in the study halls. There was a vast amount of material from previous generations of *Tannaim* that now was also organized by colleagues and students of Rabi. These works were called *breisos*—"outside" *mishnayos*. For various reasons that are not clear to us, Rabi omitted their contents from his final edition of the Mishnah. Prominent among the organizers of the *breisos* were Bar Kapara,²⁴⁶ Rabi Levi ben Sissas,²⁴⁷ Rabi Chiya and Rabi Oshiya.[248] So accepted were the *breisos* of Rabi Oshiya that in a later generation he was referred to as *Avi HaMishnah*—the "father" of the Mishnah.[249] Most of the *breisos* supply background and explanation for many of the terse and concise statements of the Mishnah; however, there are many *breisos* that clearly disagree with the decisions and conclusions of Rabi's Mishnah. Comparison of the Mishnah with the *breisos* became the standard fare of discussion in the Talmud.[250]

After the completion of the Mishnah, further works of *breisos* were organized into study books. The *breisos* that originated after the completion of the Mishnah were called *tosefta*—additions. This work of *tosefta* was also edited by Rabi Chiya and Rabi Oshiya. There was an ancient *tosefta* from the time of earlier *Tannaim*, attributed to Rabi Nechemiah,[251] but the accepted text of *tosefta* as printed today in our books of the Talmud is that of the school of Rabi Chiya and Rabi Oshiya. Thus, the *breisos* are works that preceded or were concurrent with the writing of the Mishnah, while the *tosefta* is composed of teachings that were edited after the completion of the Mishnah.[252] In the works of the later rabbinic scholars, after the completion of the Talmud, the words and works *tosefta* and *breisos* were oftentimes used interchangeably, while in the Talmud their separate identities were always preserved.[253]

When we consider the period of the writing of the Mishnah, we see that it would not have been possible without the vast powers and extraordinary talents of Rabi. As noted earlier, he put to excellent use his great wealth and diplomatic influence with the Roman authorities.[254] His superb organizational skills, impeccable royal family pedigree,[255] and his privacy and confidentiality[256] justified his postion as *Nasi*, the effective practical head of Jewish society of his time. His remarkable Torah scholarship and erudition, his sterling personal character and piety, coupled with outstanding leadership qualities made him also the *Chacham*, the head of the yeshivah. His maxim for leadership was, "One should not unnecessarily impose burdens and bother on the community"[257]—which is another reason he was so beloved.

Rabi was a person of such great personal humility that after his demise it was said that his high degree of humility was no longer in the world.[258] We witness his humble attitude in the Mishnah itself that he so painstakingly and lovingly edited: in the entire vast work, his own name and opinion appear only 34 times![259]

After every great leader, the question of succession arises. Rabi's ancestors, the descendants of Hillel, who also served as *Nasi* and head of the yeshiva, were often challenged over their dual leadership roles. The rabbis of their times objected to the concentration of too much power in the hands of one individual. This was yet an echo of the dispute that the rabbis waged against the Hasmonean kings for serving as king and High Priest at one and the same time. However, no such complaint was registered in the case of Rabi, whose greatness, holiness, humility and wisdom was of such a nature that no objection ever arose as to his dual leadership positions. Yet, in his deathbed testament, Rabi himself divided the two positions of power between two of his sons. He stated: "My son Shimon will be the *Chacham*, while my son Gamliel will become the *Nasi*."[260] He was apparently well aware of the problem of concentrating too much power and authority in one individual, even in one's own son. He also warned his sons against living in a community of scoffers, placing themselves into compromising situations, avoiding taxes and customs duties unlawfully, and exposing themselves to unnecessary dangers.[261] He then also appointed Rabi Chanina bar Chama as head of the scholars in the yeshivah.[262] Rabi was the great organizer of the Mishnah, and of Jewish society and Torah study in his day. It is no wonder that he saw to it that his succession should also be orderly and organized.

Though a great deal is known about his life, less is known of Rabi's death. As noted earlier, his original base of operation was in Beis Shearim,[263] but for the last seventeen years of his life, he lived in Tzipori.[264] He moved there because of his illnesses: the mountain air of Tzipori was beneficial to him.[265] (Tzipori's name derives from the fact that the city sits high on a mountain like a bird—*tzipor*—perched on a high place.[266]) At the time, Tzipori was a cosmopolitan and wealthy city, with a large Jewish population living side by side with Roman officialdom as well as Greek and Roman citizens.

Though it was the Greco-Roman cultural and commercial center of the Galilee, it was there that much of the work on the Mishnah was completed. Yet even after completing his monumental work in Tzipori, Rabi did not feel at home there. His dying wish was that he not be eulogized in the towns near Tzipori,[267] nor was he to buried there. Tradition tells us that he was buried in one of the large sepulchral caves at Beis Shearim,[268] though a definitive burial spot is no longer known, as is the case of many of the great men of the Mishnah. It is estimated that Rabi was in his seventies when he passed away.[269]

Rabi continued to appear to his family even after his death.[270] The trauma of Rabi's death for the Jewish people was so intense that initially the rabbis did not allow the news of his demise to be announced publicly.[271] Once publicized, the anniversary of his death was declared a fast day.[272] The rabbis characterized his death as the victory of the angels of Heaven—who bore Rabi into the World to Come—over the righteous people of this world, who implored that Rabi yet stay with them here.[273] Righteous and great people such as Rabi are in demand in both worlds. The exact year of Rabi's death is not clear: scholarly opinions range from 190 CE till as late as 220 CE.[274] It hardly matters, for Rabi remains alive and immortal until the end of time.

After Rabi, the changing of the guard in Jewish life and scholarship took place. The Mishnah is a product of the talents of those who lived in the Land of Israel, but after the death of Rabi, the center of Torah authority would switch to the Jewish communities and yeshivos of Babylonia. Though the institutions of the *Nasi* and the Sanhedrin would continue and be centered in the Land of Israel for two more centuries, the main halachic decision makers (except for matters of the calendar) would now be Jews living in Babylonia.

The prestigious yeshivos in Babylonia in the generation after Rabi were headed by his students and colleagues. Their shape and style, and their methods of Torah study and interpretation of the Mishnah, were originated by Rav and Mar Shmuel, two of the main disciples of Rabi. It was their yeshivos that set the norm for all of the Babylonian yeshivos that followed them in establishing the Talmud. They continued the work of Rabi in preserving the Oral Law and bringing its knowledge and traditions to the masses of Israel.

The yeshivos of Rav and Mar Shmuel and their derivatives existed for more than eight centuries[275] and were the mainstay of Jewish survival and accomplishment for that entire period of time. Thus, in a very real sense, Rabi should be seen as the true founder of the Babylonian Talmud. Rabi became the symbol of the never-ending continuity of Torah and Israel, and that, indeed, is the deeper meaning of the words of the Talmud that say, "On the day that Rabi died, Rav Yehudah was born."[276] Rabi is the guarantor—even in death!—of the continuity and eternity of Torah.

Rabi's two sons, Shimon and Gamliel, are mentioned many times in the Mishnah and Talmud.[277] They continued the work of their father and were zealous in preserving the family's honor and positions.[278] A story has come down to us about the time Raban Shimon's wife gave birth to a girl. Raban Shimon was disappointed, since he had wanted a boy. Rabi consoled him, but Bar Kapara shared in his disappointment.[279]

Compared to his father, our knowledge of Raban Shimon's life is a bit sketchy: He was renowned for his cleverness,[280] and he was magnanimous towards his colleagues.[281] On occasion, he accompanied his father on visits to the Roman emperor, Antoninus, when the latter was in Caesarea.[282] When he visited Rome, he was impressed by its splendor and strength, but Rabi Chiya, who accompanied him on that journey, deflated his enthusiasm for the Romans.[283] The Talmud tells us that Raban Shimon did not have a melodious voice.[284] His wedding was a famous event in the annals of the Talmud[285] because of his parents' great wealth and stature. Apparently, Rabi had daughters who were learned in *halachah*, as Raban Shimon related a *halachah* that he had heard from a sister of his in the name of their father.[286] Raban Shimon was an expert in astronomy and applied his knowledge to fixing the calendar.[287] Because of this he was called the "Candlelight of Israel,"[288] a phrase originally used to compliment and describe the great Raban Yochanan ben Zakai, generations earlier. Raban Shimon surely lived up to his father's assessment of him: He was truly the *Chacham*—the wise man and scholar—of his generation.

> **"On the day that Rabi died, Rav Yehudah was born."**
> *Kiddushin 22b*

Raban Shimon's brother, Raban Gamliel III, served as *Nasi* after the death of his father. Under his leadership, certain corrections were made in the decisions of the Mishnah because of changing circumstances. *Shechitah*—ritual slaughtering of animals and poultry—performed by *Kusim*[289] (Samaritans) was now banned by Raban Gamliel III and his colleagues, even though it had been permitted by the Mishnah.[290] It may very well be that this ruling was also addressed and applied to the Jewish Christians of the time. It was during this period—200–250 CE—that Christianity gained considerable momentum in the Roman world, and Christian attempts to convert Jews to the new faith were especially intensive. In the Talmud, we will find that the word *Kusim*, like the word *minim*, was oftentimes used as a code word for Christians.

Friendship with the Roman emperors was no longer part of the *Nasi*'s life. Raban Gamliel III warned against placing too much trust in the promises of government.[291] Public perception was always important to Raban Gamliel III and his family;[292] in fact, his sons went out of their way to avoid the impression of having committed a violation of *halachah*, even though they were convinced that no such violation truly existed.[293] Raban Gamliel III extolled the merit of public service on behalf of the Jewish people, but cautioned that one's deeds in the public sector should always be "for the sake of heaven."[294] Raban Gamliel III realized the difficulties of satisfying the public that he served, and saw that it was impossible to meet the expectations and demands of everyone.[295] He followed the dictate of his father to him "to rule decisively and with a high [i.e. strong and determined] hand."[296] Yet,

Jewish sarcophagus from Beis Shearim, first half of 4th Century CE (Collection of the Israel Antiquities Authority)

he always preached the supremacy of mercy and tolerance towards others.[297] In advising his students, he encouraged them to pursue a gainful occupation in order to be self-sufficient.[298]

With the end of the reign of Rabi's two sons, the work of the Mishnah can be seen as completed and sealed. The world surrounding the Jewish people was changing, and not for the better. Rome would become engaged in a bitter inner struggle with Christianity for the entire next century, until finally Constantine (in the fourth century) would convert the empire to this newly ascendant faith. The struggle of Rome with Christianity would worsen the situation of the Jews in the Land of Israel, since the Jews did not support either side in this bloody dispute and were thus viewed with hostility by both sides.

The Jewish community in the Land of Israel dwindled in numbers and in influence. Babylonia became a safer haven for Torah study and Jewish continuity due to its providential, almost inexplicable, isolation from both Christianity and Roman rule. The Mishnah, produced in the Land of Israel, was Hebrew and holy, written in light and conciseness and simplicity—for the Land itself bespeaks light and simplicity. The main Talmud was a product of the exile and Babylonia. The exile, by nature, is very complicated and has much more shade than light in its environs. The Talmud is also holy; nevertheless, it was written in Aramaic and darkness.[299] It is complicated and verbose, wide-ranging and all encompassing.

But it is the Torah—and only the Torah—that flourishes in all environments and under all circumstances. The great men of the Mishnah, the *Tannaim* whose lives and achievements we have been privileged to glimpse and record on the pages of this book, remain the saviors of Israel in all generations and climes. The Mishnah is not only knowledge; it is inspiration as well. And inspiration is found not only in ideas: it is gained from people. If any reader of this book—hopefully now enlightened on the lives of the creators of the Mishnah—will feel inspired to look at the Mishnah more closely due to this book, I will feel amply rewarded for all of the efforts and time expended in writing it.

A final word needs to be said. All of the people described in this book are superhuman characters to us. In our generation, we have never met anyone of their stature or kind. Even though the Talmud portrays their lives in a matter-of-fact way (hence, being faithful to its Talmudic sources, this book also does not always deal in superlatives), these people are far from ordinary humans. The shadow of their lives and the immensity of their achievements reach down to touch each and every one of us today.

The Talmud itself wished for us to know the story of their lives, otherwise it would not have devoted so much space and detail in recording these events and personalities for us. It is in the tradition of Torah learning itself—*drosh v'kabel schar*, learn and study and thereby acquire merit—that the lives of these great people are outlined for us. They set a standard of human achievement for us, and even though we cannot reach, or in many instances even understand, their spiritual levels and attainments, it is important to know that such a standard does, in fact, exist.

The Talmud does not allow us, God forbid, to judge or assess their behavior from our limited perspective. It wishes that we recognize and have knowledge of their lives and struggles so that we may gain merit by knowing that such people once inhabited Jewish society and laid the foundation for all later Jewish scholarship—and for Jewish survival itself. And by knowing their stories as outlined in the Talmud, we can come to know, appreciate and love them. The people of the Mishnah are our true heroes and exemplary role models. It is because of them that Jews have always felt that every generation and circumstance is "a time for God."

APPENDICES

Shishah Sidrei Mishnah

ZERAIM: *laws relating to agriculture*

Tractates	Mishnah Chapters	Talmud Bavli	Talmud Yerushalmi
Berachos	9	•	•
Peah	8		•
Demai	8		•
Kilayim	9		•
Shevi'is	10		•
Terumos	11		•
Maasros	5		•
Maaser Sheini	5		•
Challah	4		•
Orlah	3		•
Bikurim	3		•

MOED: *laws relating to Shabbos and holy days of the Jewish calendar*

Tractates	Mishnah Chapters	Talmud Bavli	Talmud Yerushalmi
Shabbos	24	•	•
Eiruvin	10	•	•
Pesachim	10	•	•
Shekalim	8	•	•
Yoma	8	•	•
Sukkah	5	•	•
Beitzah	5	•	•
Rosh Hashanah	4	•	•
Taanis	4	•	•
Megillah	4	•	•
Moed Katan	3	•	•
Chagigah	3	•	•

NASHIM: *laws relating to the relationships between men and women*

Tractates	Mishnah Chapters	Talmud Bavli	Talmud Yerushalmi
Yevamos	16	•	•
Kesubos	13	•	•
Nedarim	11	•	•
Nazir	9	•	•
Sotah	9	•	•
Gittin	9	•	•
Kiddushin	4	•	•

NEZIKIN: *Laws relating to civil law, criminal law & judicial proceedings*

Tractates	Mishnah Chapters	Talmud Bavli	Talmud Yerushalmi
Bava Kama	10	•	•
Bava Metzia	10	•	•
Bava Basra	10	•	•
Sanhedrin	11	•	•
Makkos	3	•	•
Shevuos	8	•	•
Eduyos	8		
Avodah Zarah	5	•	•
Avos	5		
Horayos	3	•	•

KODASHIM: *Laws relating to temple sacrifices and dietary laws*

Tractates	Mishnah Chapters	Talmud Bavli	Talmud Yerushalmi
Zevachim	14	•	
Menachos	13	•	
Chullin	12	•	
Bechoros	9	•	
Arachin	9	•	
Temurah	7	•	
Kereisos	6	•	
Meilah	6	•	
Tamid	6	•	
Midos	5		
Kinnim	3		

TAHAROS: *Laws relating to ritual purity in the temple and the home*

Tractates	Mishnah Chapters	Talmud Bavli	Talmud Yerushalmi
Keilim	30		
Oholos	18		
Negaim	14		
Parah	12		
Taharos	10		
Mikvaos	10		
Niddah	10	•	•
Machshirin	6		
Zavim	5		
Tvul-Yom	4		
Yadayim	4		
Oktzin	3		

Tannaim Timeline

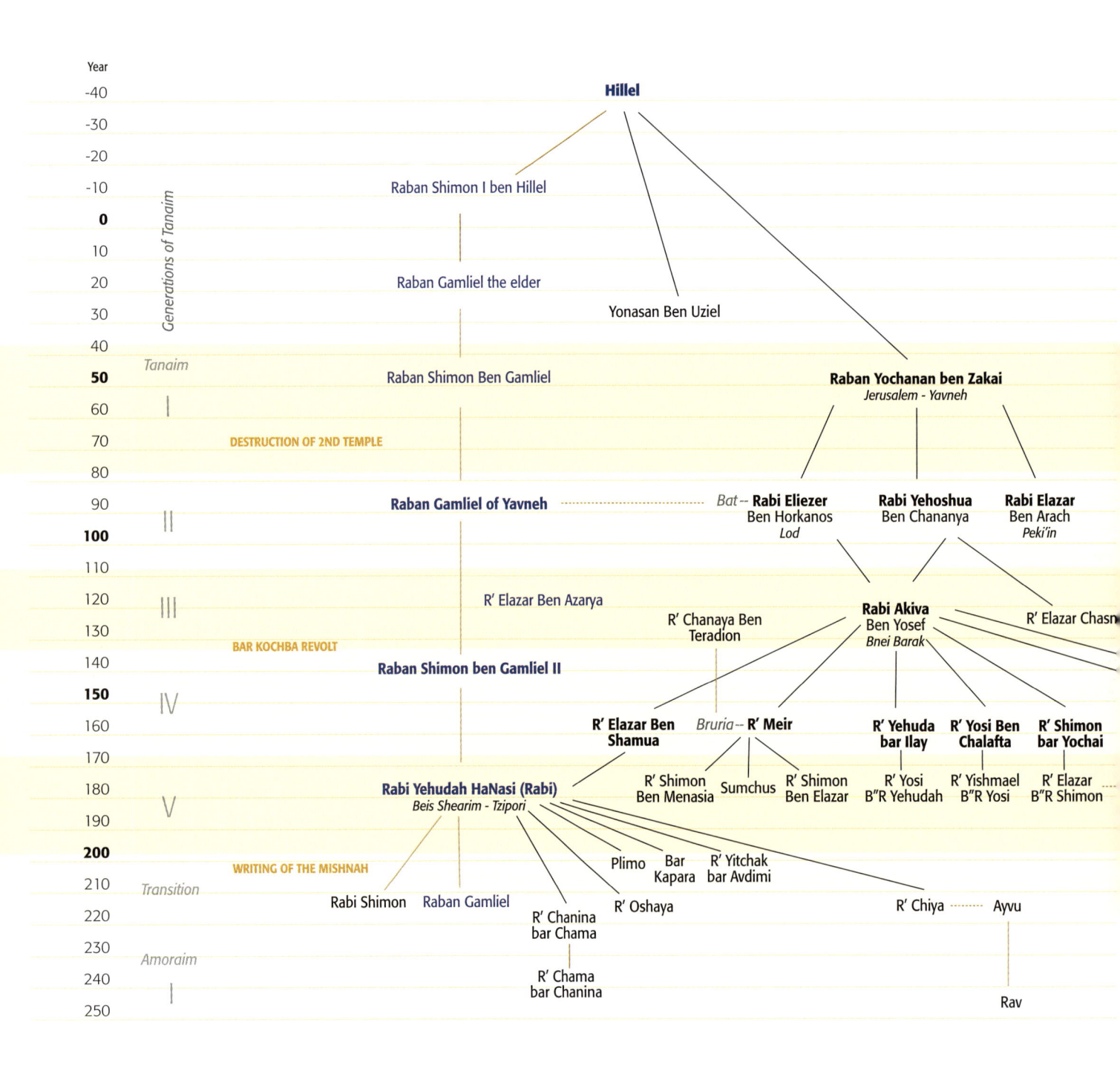

Year	Generations of Tanaim							
-40			**Hillel**					
-30								
-20								
-10		Raban Shimon I ben Hillel						
0								
10								
20		Raban Gamliel the elder						
30			Yonasan Ben Uziel					
40								
50	Tanaim I	Raban Shimon Ben Gamliel		**Raban Yochanan ben Zakai** *Jerusalem - Yavneh*				
60								
70	DESTRUCTION OF 2ND TEMPLE							
80								
90	II	**Raban Gamliel of Yavneh** .... *Bat*--	**Rabi Eliezer** Ben Horkanos *Lod*	**Rabi Yehoshua** Ben Chananya	**Rabi Elazar** Ben Arach *Peki'in*			
100								
110								
120	III	R' Elazar Ben Azarya	R' Chanaya Ben Teradion	**Rabi Akiva** Ben Yosef *Bnei Barak*	R' Elazar Chasm			
130								
140	BAR KOCHBA REVOLT	**Raban Shimon ben Gamliel II**						
150	IV							
160			**R' Elazar Ben Shamua**	*Bruria*-- **R' Meir**	**R' Yehuda bar Ilay**	**R' Yosi Ben Chalafta**	**R' Shimon bar Yochai**	
170				R' Shimon Ben Menasia / Sumchus / R' Shimon Ben Elazar	R' Yosi B"R Yehuda	R' Yishmael B"R Yosi	R' Elazar B"R Shimon	
180	V	**Rabi Yehudah HaNasi (Rabi)** *Beis Shearim - Tzipori*						
190								
200		WRITING OF THE MISHNAH	Plimo / Bar Kapara / R' Yitzchak bar Avdimi					
210	Transition	Rabi Shimon / Raban Gamliel	R' Oshaya		R' Chiya .... Ayvu			
220			R' Chanina bar Chama					
230	Amoraim I							
240			R' Chama bar Chanina		Rav			
250								

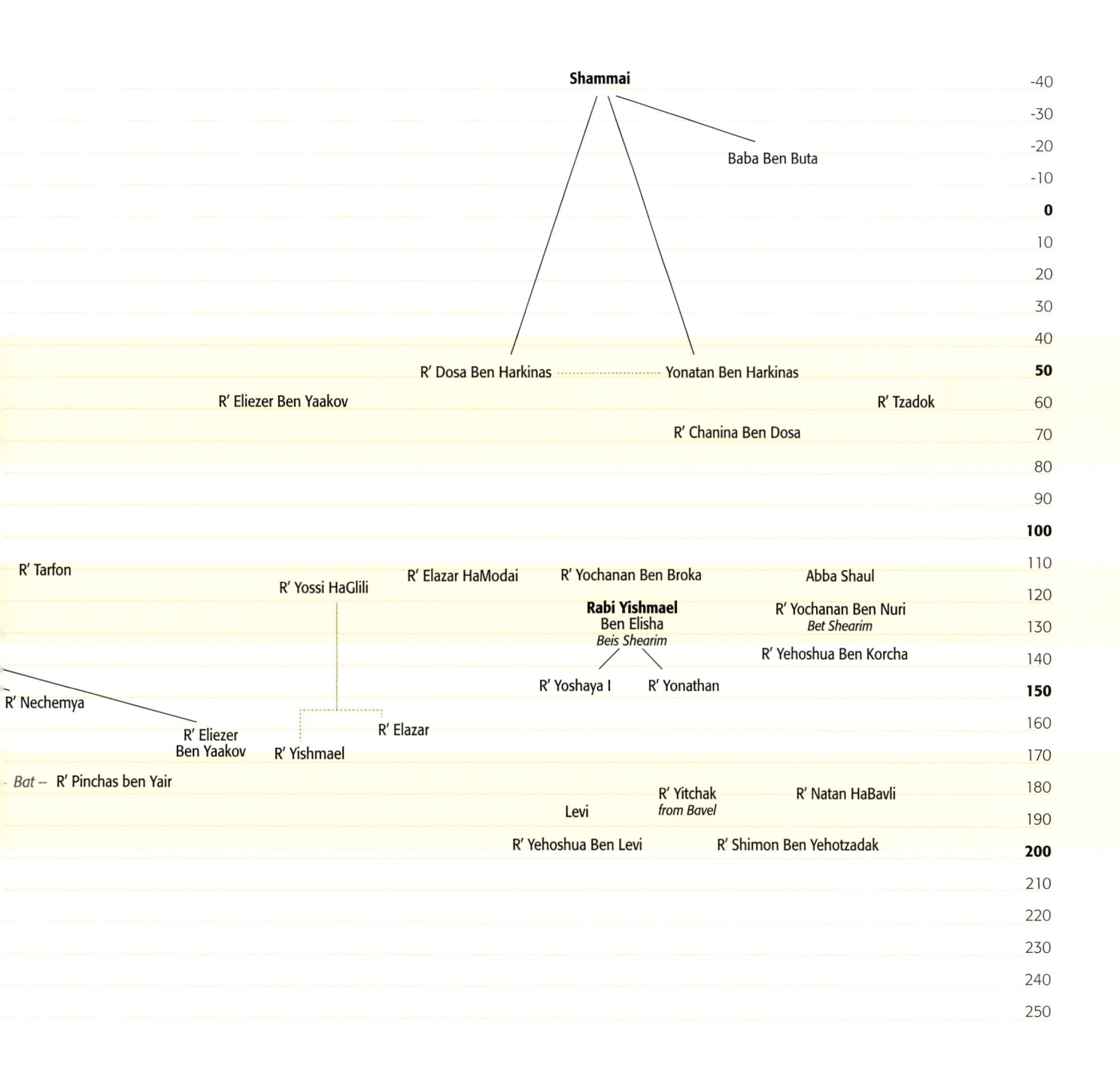

	Year
Shammai	-40
	-30
Baba Ben Buta	-20
	-10
	0
	10
	20
	30
	40
R' Dosa Ben Harkinas ········ Yonatan Ben Harkinas	**50**
R' Eliezer Ben Yaakov · · · · · · · · R' Tzadok	60
R' Chanina Ben Dosa	70
	80
	90
	100
R' Tarfon	110
R' Yossi HaGlili · · · R' Elazar HaModai · · · R' Yochanan Ben Broka · · · Abba Shaul	120
Rabi Yishmael Ben Elisha · · · R' Yochanan Ben Nuri *Bet Shearim*	130
Beis Shearim · · · R' Yehoshua Ben Korcha	140
R' Yoshaya I · · · R' Yonathan	**150**
R' Nechemya	160
R' Eliezer Ben Yaakov · · · R' Yishmael · · · R' Elazar	170
Bat -- R' Pinchas ben Yair	180
Levi · · · R' Yitchak *from Bavel* · · · R' Natan HaBavli	190
R' Yehoshua Ben Levi · · · R' Shimon Ben Yehotzadak	**200**
	210
	220
	230
	240
	250

Legend:
- blue text — Nasi
- ——— Student
- ——— Parent-child
- ·········· Sibling
- -- Spouse

Notes

Section I

1. Megillah 16b.
2. Sanhedrin 21b.
3. Shir HaShirim Rabah, chapter 5, section 5.
4. Menachos 53a.
5. *Avos D'Rabi Nosson*, chapter 13.
6. Gittin 60b. Also see Reuven Margoliyus, *Yesod HaMishnah V'arichasa* (Jerusalem: Mosad Harav Kook, Fourth Edition, Tel Aviv, 1956), pp. 4-7 and accompanying footnotes, for a scholarly and thorough review of these early *megillos*. As an example, he points out there that the entire series of *Mishnayos* that comprise the fifth chapter of tractate Zevachim in the Mishnah was written down in its final form even before the building of the Second Temple! That accounts for the fact that in this entire chapter of the Mishnah, no differences of opinion are recorded. In fact, it was this ancient written *megillah* that was incorporated whole and verbatim into the Mishnah centuries later, and which formed the basic knowledge as to how to recreate the Temple service at the time of Ezra.
7. Margoliyus, ibid.
8. Ibid.
9. Yoma 69a.
10. Yoma 39a-b. The Talmud records the miracles that regularly occurred during the 40 years of his reign as *Kohein Gadol*—High Priest. These miracles related to the lots that decided the scapegoat, the western lamp on the great candelabra, the fire on the altar, the blessing inherent in the showbread and the offering of the two loaves of Shavuos, and other facets of Temple service. After his death, these miracles were no longer constant.
11. Nedarim 9b.
12. Menachos 109b. See there the discussion between the rabbis as to whether this Temple was meant to serve the God of Israel or became a place of pagan service.
13. Yoma 9a.
14. Mishnah Parah, chapter 3, mishnah 5, Tiferes Yisrael there, note 9.
15. Avos, chapter 1, mishnah 2.
16. Yoma 39a-b.
17. Tosefos Sotah 38a.
18. Rabbi Yosef Kapach, trans. and ed., *Perush HaRambam l'Mishnah* (Jerusalem: Mosad HaRav Kook 1964), volume 1, p. 28.
19. Yevamos 16a. See also Gittin 81a, where Rabi Dosa is identified as beginning the period of *doros achronim*—the later generations of the people of the Mishnah, in contrast to the Houses of Shammai and Hillel who were the earlier generations.
20. For instance, see Eliezer Shteinman, *Be'er HaTalmud* (Tel Aviv: Masada Press, 1967) volume 1, p. 278.
21. Talmud Yerushalmi, at the conclusion of Maseches Sotah. See also Moed Katan 26a, where King Saul is called *Nasi* and his son Yehonasan is titled *Av Beis Din*, the titles used in the description of the *Zugos*.

22. Avos, chapter 1, mishnah 2.
23. *Avos D'Rabi Nosson,* chapter 5, section 2.
24. Megillah 9a; Megillas Taanis; Sofrim, chapter 1, section 7.
25. Chagigah 16b; Rabeinu Menachem HaMeiri, *Introduction to Maseches Avos* (Jerusalem: Machon HaTalmud HaYisraeli HaShalem, Yad Harav Herzog) 1964, p. 22.
26. See Margoliyus, p. 7, note 12.
27. Shabbos 14b.
28. Bava Basra 133b.
29. Bereshis Rabah, Midrash Hamfoar edition, chapter 65, section 22.
30. Ibid.
31. Chagigah 16a.
32. See Rashi, Sotah 47a, "Haeshkolos." See also T'murah 15b.
33. Sanhedrin 107b, in the uncensored version.
34. Menachos 109b.
35. See Sanhedrin 107b, in the uncensored version, for the story of Yehoshua ben Prachyah and his student, Yeshu. Most commentators agree that the cryptic and strange story that appears there hides much more than it reveals.
36. Tosefta Machshirim, chapter 3, section 4.
37. Avos, chapter one, mishnah 6 and 7.
38. Chagigah 16b; Tosefta Chagigah, chapter 2, section 8.
39. Yerushalmi Berachos, chapter 7, halachah 2.
40. Berachos 48a. See also Sanhedrin 19a and b regarding the unsuccessful attempt of Shimon to try Alexander Yanai for murder before the Sanhedrin.
41. Kiddushin 66a.
42. Megillas Taanis, chapter 9.
43. Yerushalmi Chagigah, chapter 2, section 2.
44. Makkos 5b.
45. Avos, chapter 1, mishnah 8.
46. Yerushalmi Kesubos, chapter 8, halachah 11. And see *Korban Edah* there saying that, originally, fathers taught their children, but when that system broke down, Shimon ben Shatach established a general school system beginning from age six or seven.
47. Shabbos 14b and see Yerushalmi Kesubos, chapter 8, halachah 11. See also Kesubos 82b.
48. Berachos 19a.
49. Taanis, chapter 3, mishnah 8.
50. Taanis 23a.
51. Midrash Rabah, Devarim, chapter 3, section 5.
52. See Sanhedrin 45b; Yerushalmi Sanhedrin, chapter 6, halachah 6; Yerushalmi Chagigah, chapter 2, halachah 2; and Rashi, Sanhedrin 44b, "Dbaya." See also, Shteinman, volume 1, p. 57, that Shimon could not save his son because the people would view that as favoritism and corruption of the justice system.
53. Sotah 49b; Menachos 64b. Also Bava Kama 82b, where the Talmud intimates that it was Aristoblus besieging Yehudah Hyrkan and not vice versa.
54. Avos, chapter 1, mishnah 10.
55. See the commentary of Rabbi Ovadyah of Bartenura to Eduyos, chapter 1, mishnah 3, "Shechayav." See also Yoma 71b, where they were addressed as being "sons of the (non-Jewish) nations."
56. Inferred in Gittin 57b.
57. Ibid.
58. Pesachim 70b.

59. Josephus Flavius, *Antiquities of the Jews*, book 14, chapter 9, section 4.
60. *Avos D'Rabi Nosson*, chapter 11, mishnah 1.
61. Chagigah 16a.
62. For examples, see Shabbos 15a; Beitzah 25a; Yevamos 67a; Eduyos, chapter 1, mishnah 3; Yerushalmi Sotah, chapter 2, halachah 5.
63. See Succah 20a and Sotah 48b.
64. Ibid. Succah.
65. Yerushalmi Taanis, chapter 4, halachah 2.
66. Yoma 35b.
67. Ibid.
68. Ibid.
69. Sotah 21a.
70. Sofrim, chapter 16, section 9.
71. See Margoliyus, p. 8. See also Yitzchak Isaac Halevi, *Doros HaRishonim*, section 2 (Warsaw, 1896), pp. 25-31 that the Sanhedrin itself disbanded at that time and that the Bnei Bseira ruled on their own. Thus, they were able to relinquish their authority and power to Hillel unilaterally without the approval of the Sanhedrin, since the latter body no longer functioned.
72. Chagigah 16b.
73. Ibid.
74. Ibid.
75. Chagigah 16a.
76. Ibid.
77. Pesachim 66a. See also Margoliyus, p. 47, for an interesting discussion as to this very mysterious matter as to why Bnei Bseira did not know how to deal with the issue. See also Yerushalmi Kilayim, chapter 9, halachah 3, where Rabi Yehudah HaNasi, one of the humblest of all men, admits that he would be unable to reach the level of humility of Bnei Bseira in voluntarily relinquishing their position to Hillel.
78. Tosefta Sanhedrin, chapter 7, section 11; *Avos D'Rabi Nosson*, chapter 37, section 10.
79. Shabbos 15a. However, see Yerushalmi Chagigah, chapter 2, halachah 2 that they disputed four matters. Perhaps the difference is whether the original long-standing dispute over the placing of hands on the holiday sacrificial animal is counted, and if their disputes included not only that issue, but three new matters as well.
80. See Margoliyus, p. 44, where he states that the *Av Beis Din* had a veto right over the halachic decisions of the *Nasi* and therefore the matter could not be settled, since every *Av Beis Din* in those generations exercised that veto right.
81. See Rabeinu Menachem Hameiri, *Introduction to Maseches Avos*, p. 23. "Then [at the time of Hillel and Shammai] the light of wisdom began to dim and many more things [of Torah knowledge] became hidden and disputes [in halachah] began to multiply."
82. *Avos D'Rabi Nosson*, chapter 2, section 9.
83. Pesachim 66a. See also footnote 51 above.
84. See the famous incidents with Hillel's converts in Shabbos 31a and in greater detail in *Avos D'Rabi Nosson*, chapter 15, section 2.
85. Ibid. Shabbos 31a and *Avos D'Rabi Nosson*.
86. Ibid.
87. Ibid.
88. Ibid.
89. Berachos 60a.

90. Avos, chapter 2, mishnah 7.
91. Ibid., mishnah 8.
92. Ibid., mishnah 6.
93. Ibid., mishnah 4.
94. Beitzah 16a.
95. Pesachim 66a.
96. Sifrei, Zos HaBrachah, section 357 records that Hillel lived as long as Moses, 120 years.
97. Sanhedrin 5a.
98. Sanhedrin 11a.
99. Ibid.
100. Shabbos 31a.
101. Beitzah 16a.
102. Succah, chapter 2, mishnah 8.
103. Chagigah 16a. See Shteinman, volume 1, p. 207, for theories as to who Menachem was and why he retired. The Talmud Chagigah offers differing opinions as to what Menachem did after leaving his post. See note 75 above.
104. Yevamos 14a.
105. Yerushalmi Shabbos, chapter 1, halachah 4. See also Shabbos 17a.
106. Beis Shammai was of the opinion that the majority was not to be judged in quantity—numbers; but rather in quality—intellect and merit. See Margoliyus, pp. 9-11, 49-50 and the footnotes there.
107. Eiruvin 13b.
108. See, for example, Shabbos 13b and the continuation of the discussion there in the Talmud.
109. Shabbos 17a.
110. Eiruvin 13b.
111. Sotah 47b.
112. Berachos 36b.
113. See Tosefta at the beginning of Eduyos, that when the rabbis arrived at Yavneh after the Temple's destruction and began to develop the Mishnah, they stated, "Let us begin from Hillel and Shammai."
114. See Margoliyus, p. 57 onwards for a full discussion of this.
115. Ibid.
116. His son, Shimon, his grandson, Raban Gamliel the Elder, and his great-grandson, Rabi Shimon ben Gamliel I, all occupied the position of *Nasi* until the destruction of the Temple. The dynasty of Hillel and his descendants serving as *Nasi* of Israel lasted for fifteen generations!
117. Eiruvin 13b.
118. Mishnah Shevees, chapter 10, mishnah 3 and 4; Arachin, chapter 9, mishnah 4; Avodah Zarah 36b; Shabbos 13b-15a.
119. Bava Kama 79b.
120. Avos, chapter 1, mishnah 13. Also, Avos, chapter 2, mishnah 4.
121. Pesachim 115a.
122. Sanhedrin 11a.
123. Shteinman, volume 1, p. 218.

Section II

1. Shabbos 15a.
2. Yerushalmi Berachos, chapter 9, section 3.
3. Reuven Margoliyus, *Yesod HaMishnah V'arichasa* (Jerusalem: Mosad Harav Kook, Fourth Edition, Tel Aviv, 1956) p. 13, note 31, is of the opinion that Shimon was already 90 years old when he assumed office.
4. Avraham Moshe Naftal, *HaTalmud V'yotzrav*, volume 2 (Tel Aviv: Yavneh Publishing House, 1972) p. 120.
5. Margoliyus, p. 13, note 32. Also note that Rabeinu Nissim of tenth-century Kairouan, Morocco, wrote that the title "*Raban*" was reserved for the descendants of Hillel who were of the House of David by matrilineal descent, whereas the Exilarchs of Babylonia who were called "*Ravna*" were of the House of David by virtue of patrilineal descent. See Reuven Margoliyus, *L'Cheker Sheimos V'Kinuyim BaTalmud* (Jerusalem: Mosad Harav Kook,1989), p. 55.
6. Naftal on page 241 of volume 1 assigns him to the generation immediately after Raban Gamliel I. However, the Talmud (Semachos, chapter 8) has Raban Gamliel I eulogizing him after Shmuel HaKatan's death. See Yisrael Konovitz, *Maarchaos Tannaim* (Jerusalem: Mosad Harav Kook, 1967), volume 1, p. 271. Others say that the correct interpretation there is Raban Gamliel II of Yavneh (though the text in Semachos reads Raban Gamliel HaZaken) and that Shmuel HaKatan lived a very long life, surviving long after Raban Gamliel I. See Eliezer Shteinman, *Be'er HaTalmud* (Tel Aviv: Masada Press, 1967), p. 267.
7. Berachos 28b.
8. Pesachim 88b.
9. See Eiruvin 64b, where there is a difference of opinion two generations after the death of Raban Gamliel I as to what his true attitude was toward the Saducees, its effect on his halachic rulings and their consequences towards them, even when treating them as individuals.
10. Semachos chapter 8.
11. Sotah 49a.
12. Tosefta, Shabbos, chapter 7, section 18.
13. Semachos, chapter 8.
14. See Rashi, Shabbos 13b, in his comment regarding Megillas Taanis.
15. Kesuvos 8b; Moed Katan 27b.
16. Yerushalmi Sanhedrin, chapter 1, section 2.
17. Rosh Hashanah 23b; Eiruvin 45a; Sanhedrin 11a.
18. Yevamos 122a.
19. Gittin 34b; Gittin 36a; Yerushalmi Bava Basra, chapter 10, section 4.
20. Gittin 34b.
21. Brachos 28b.
22. Niddah 6b; Kesuvos 10b.
23. Yerushalmi Sotah, chapter 9, section 13.
24. Avos, chapter 4, mishnah 19.
25. Sanhedrin 11a.
26. Shabbos 33a.
27. Sanhedrin 11a.
28. Semachos, chapter 8.
29. Ibid.
30. And perhaps after, as well. See note 6 above.

31. Eduyos, chapter 5, section 6.
32. Ibid.
33. Ibid. See there also the opinion that Akavya never was banned, but it was a different person who was the object of the rabbinic ban. See also Sifra, Bamidbar 12:9, where it also states that Akavya was never banned.
34. Yerushalmi Sanhedrin, chapter 8, section 1. See also Eduyos, chapter 5, section 7, where Akavya instructs his own son to follow the rule of the majority and not to maintain his father's positions in the halachic dispute with the other members of the Sanhedrin.
35. Chapter 3, section 1.
36. Eduyos, chapter 5, section 7.
37. See Midrash Tanchuma, Shmos, section 2; Pesachim 14a-b; Parah, chapter 3, section 1; Yoma, 39a; Eduyos, chapter 2, section 3.
38. Avos D'Rabi Nosson, chapter 20, section 1.
39. Megillas Taanis, at the end of the book.
40. Succah 28a.
41. Sanhedrin 41a.
42. Yevamos 49b.
43. See Shteinman, volume 1, p. 240.
44. Kesubos 104b.
45. Kesubos 105a.
46. Peah, chapter 2, mishnah 6; Yoma 14b. He was yet a member of the Sanhedrin when it still met in the precincts of the Temple.
47. Ibid., in Peah.
48. Yoma 18b. He was an eyewitness to the service of the High Priest in the Temple and participated in studying with him on the night of Yom Kippur so that he would not fall asleep.
49. Beitzah 29a; Shabbos 157a. In Beitzah 29a, his scrupulous behavior regarding weights and measures is emphasized. Nevertheless, we find in Yerushalmi Beitzah, chapter 3, his complaint that even though he was so scrupulous and honest, he still could not escape physical pain. See also Pesachim 57a, for his strong condemnation of injustices and nepotism perpetrated by the wealthy and mighty.
50. Pesachim 3b. He claimed to have been descended from the "dead bones" that the prophet Yechezkel revived. See Sanhedrin 92b.
51. Tosefta, Keilim, Bava Kama, chapter 1, section 6. Apparently, he once entered the Temple without proper purification, for which he was later reprimanded by Rabi Eliezer.
52. Shabbos 15a.
53. Succah 53a.
54. Sotah 49b; Bava Kama, 83a.
55. Sotah 49b; Bava Kama, 83a.
56. Mechilta, Shmos, chapter 22, section 22; Avos D'Rabi Nosson, chapter 38, section 3.
57. Chapter 1, mishnah 17.
58. Kesubos 61b.
59. Yerushalmi Taanis, chapter 3, section 10. A similar type of confrontation between Choni and Rabi Shimon ben Shatach is recorded in Taanis 19a. Since Choni lived a very long life, having at one point slept for 70 consecutive years, it certainly is possible that he encountered the criticisms of both Shimons as recorded in both of the above Talmuds.
60. Bava Basra 166a; Krisus 8a.

61. Bava Basra 134a; Bava Basra 134a; Yerushalmi Nedarim, chapter 5, section 6; Avos D'Rabi Nosson, chapter 14, section 1.
62. Pesachim 3b.
63. Sanhedrin 41a.
64. See Succah 28a as to his Torah greatness.
65. Ibid.
66. Berachos 17a.
67. Sanhedrin 32b.
68. Avos, chapter 2, mishnah 9.
69. Succah 28a.
70. Ibid.
71. Ibid.
72. Ibid.
73. Yerushalmi Taanis, chapter 3, section 11; Bava Basra 10a; Chagigah 14b.
74. Bava Basra 89b.
75. Seder Eliyahu Zuta, chapter 17.
76. This was unlike the opinion of Rabi Akiva and Rabi Yochanan, and others, who in later times used others' personal tragedies as a source of comfort to the newly bereaved.
77. Avos D'Rabi Nosson, chapter 14, section 6.
78. Ibid., chapter 25.
79. Seder Eliyahu Zuta, chapter 17.
80. Gittin 56a-b.
81. Yoma 39b; Avos D'Rabi Nosson, chapter 31.
82. Avos D'Rabi Nosson, chapter 4, section 5.
83. Ibid.
84. Gittin 56a-b.
85. Ibid.
86. Ibid. For a variant reading of the meeting and Raban Yochanan's requests, see Avos D'Rabi Nosson, chapter 4, section 5. For a breathtakingly beautiful interpretation of the requests of Raban Yochanan and the scene, see Shteinman, volume 1, pp. 243-244.
87. Gittin 56b.
88. Ibid.
89. Yerushalmi Sanhedrin, chapter 1, section 2; Bechoros 5a.
90. Bamidbar Rabah, chapter 19, section 4.
91. Bava Basra 115b-116a; Mishnah Yadayim, chapter 4, section 6; Tosefta Parah, chapter 3, section 4.
92. Bamidbar Rabah, chapter 19, section 4.
93. Ibid.
94. Eduyos, chapter 8, section 7. See also Succah 28a that Raban Yochanan ben Zakai never stated a Torah matter that he had not previously heard from his teachers!
95. Sifra Bamidbar, Chukas, chapter 19, section 2; Tosefta Oholos, chapter 16, sections 7 and 8; Tosefta Parah, chapter 4, section 7.
96. They are discussed mainly in the fourth chapter of Rosh Hashanah from folio 29b onward.
97. Sanhedrin 32b; Yerushalmi Maasros, chapter 2, section 2; Maaser Rishon, chapter 2, section 1.
98. See Shteinman, volume 1, pp. 251-255 for a beautiful description of Raban Yochanan's personality and character. See also Yitzchak Isaac Halevi, *Doros*

HaRishonim (Warsaw, 1896), book 1, volume 5, beginning on p. 52 for a description of Raban Gamliel being the *Nasi* and Raban Yochanan ben Zakai deferring to him in that role.

99. Yerushalmi Horayos, chapter 3, section 2; Toras Kohanim (Sifra), Vayikra 4:22.
100. Mechilta Yisro 20:22; section 8.
101. Tosefta Bava Kama, chapter 7, section 6.
102. Mechilta D'Rabi Shimon ben Yochai, Yisro 20:22.
103. Bava Basra 10b.
104. Eduyos, chapter 8, mishnah 7.
105. Tosefta Bava Kama, chapter 7, section 5.
106. Bava Kama 79b.
107. Shteinman, p. 259.
108. Tosefta Sotah, chapter 15, section II.
109. Avos D'Rabi Nosson, chapter 4.
110. This Jewish philosopher wrote a spirited defense of Judaism and a refutation of Flaccum's basic charges against the Jews. He called it *Im Flaccum*.
111. Josephus Flavius, *Wars of the Jews*, book 2, chapter 18, sections 7 and 8.
112. Avos, chapter 2, mishnah 10.
113. Naftal, volume 1, pp. 35, 65.
114. Midrash Rabah, Koheles, chapter 7, section 15.
115. Avos D'Rabi Nosson, at the conclusion of chapter 14.
116. Sanhedrin 92b: Yechezkel, chapter 37.
117. Rosh Hashanah 29b. See also Halevi, book 1, volume 5, p. 190 and onward.
118. For instance, Tractates Yoma, and Tamid are assigned in the Talmud (Yoma 14b; Yerushalmi Yoma, chapter 2, section 2) to the authorship of Rabi Shimon ish HaMitzpeh, a contemporary of Rabi Yochanan ben Zakai. Tractate Midos is assigned in the Talmud to the authorship to Rabi Eliezer ben Yaakov I (Yoma 16a), also an elder at the time of Raban Yochanan ben Zakai. Also, chapters in the Mishnah were added to other tractates to record eyewitness memories of the Temple, events that happened during its time, and customs (for example, chapter 5 of Succah and chapter 3 in Parah).
119. Taanis 29a. See Halevi, book 1, volume 5, p. 76 and Naftal, volume 1, p. 30, both of whom state that the name of the Roman commander mentioned there in the Talmud should be Terentius Rufus and not Tineius Rufus. The latter was the Roman commander who ordered the execution of Rabi Akiva a number of decades after the passing of Raban Gamliel II.
120. Ibid. Naftal, p. 41.
121. Yerushalmi Sanhedrin, chapter 7, section 13.
122. See Bereshis Rabah, chapter 42, section 1.
123. Berachos 28a.
124. Bava Metzia 59b.
125. Avos D'Rabi Nosson, chapter 6, section 3.
126. Ibid. See one opinion there that he actually was reduced to eating dirt and picking through dung to survive!
127. Avos, chapter 2, mishnah 11, according to one opinion in that mishnah.
128. Ibid. Avos D'Rabi Nosson.
129. Taanis 25b.
130. Bereshis Rabah, Vayetze, section 70.
131. Bava Metzia 59b.
132. Sanhedrin 68a.
133. Sanhedrin 32b.

134. Yerushalmi Sanhedrin, chapter 7, section 13.
135. Yerushalmi Avodah Zarah, chapter 16, section 2; chapter 17, section 1.
136. Bava Metzia 59b.
137. Ibid.
138. Avos D'Rabi Nosson, chapter 25, section 3.
139. Ibid., chapter 16, section 2.
140. Ibid.
141. Sanhedrin 101a.
142. Avos D'Rabi Nosson, chapter 25, section 3.
143. Sanhedrin 68a.
144. Ibid; Kallah Rabasi, chapter 6.
145. Sotah 49b.
146. Sanhedrin 68a.
147. Bava Kama 74b.
148. Yerushalmi Yevamos, chapter 1, section 6.
149. Avos, chapter 2, mishnah 8.
150. Avos D'Rabi Nosson, chapter 14, section 3.
151. Maasros, chapter 2, section 2.
152. For example, see Shabbos 12a.
153. Shabbos 139a; Tosefta Eduyos, chapter 1.
154. Halevi, section 1, volume 5, p. 138 and onwards.
155. Naftal, volume 1, chapter 2.
156. Margoliyus, birurim 8, p. 51 onwards.
157. Naftal, p. 49.
158. Rosh Hashanah 25a.
159. Rabenu Chananel in his commentary there in Rosh Hashanah.
160. Naftal, p. 50.
161. Berachos 27b.
162. Beitzah 6a.
163. Hillel's wise admonition in Avos, chapter 2, mishnah 5, "Never say something to someone that you do not want to be known publicly, for in the end your words will be heard [by all]" was again proven correct in these incidents of Rabi Yehoshua with Raban Gamliel.
164. Naftal, p. 51.
165. Margoliyus, pp. 52-53.
166. Bechoros 36a.
167. Berachos 27b.
168. Shabbos 11a.
169. Margoliyus, pp. 52-53.
170. Ibid.
171. Rabi Akiva was disappointed at not being chosen and ruefully bemoaned his lack of pedigree as the cause.
172. It may have been that he was not yet placed in *cherem*—banned—at the time of this incident.
173. Margoliyus, p. 53.
174. Tradition makes him either 18 or 21 years old at the time. See Berachos 27b. He aged quickly though, soon bearing the appearance of a 70-year-old person. Being a leader of the Jewish people can do that to you rather easily.
175. Berachos 28a.
176. See Margoliyus, p. 43, note 3, for a beautiful exposition of this fact.
177. The entire exposition and description of "that day" and its incidents and

participants is recorded for us in Berachos 28a.
178. Berachos 28a.
179. See Chagigah 3a: "Whose week was it?"
180. Ibid.
181. Halevi, p. 296 onwards. See also Naftal, pp. 66-67.
182. See Yevamos 14b and 15a that a significant halachic matter could not be resolved because "the time necessary to adjudicate it was destroyed [by the fear of the Romans]."
183. Bava Kama 83a. There is a difference of opinion as to this being Rabban Gamliel HaZaken or Rabban Gamliel of Yavneh. See note 54 above.
184. Rosh Hashanah 32b and see Yerushalmi Rosh Hashanah, chapter 4, section 8. See Halevi, pp. 345-346, who ascribes these events to the time of Domitian.
185. Eiruvin 101b; Shabbos 115a.
186. Tosefta Sanhedrin, chapter 2, section 13. See also Shabbos 115a and Yerushalmi Sanhedrin, chapter 1, section 2.
187. Tosefta Terumos, chapter 2, section 13.
188. Ibid.
189. Naftal, volume 2, p. 76.
190. Succah 23a and 41b.
191. Avodah Zarah 54b and 55a.
192. Avodah Zarah 11a; Gitin 56b.
193. Yerushalmi Bava Kama, chapter 4, section 3; Sifrei Devarim, Zos HaBrachah, section 344.
194. Rosh Hashanah 31a-b.
195. Tosefta Pesachim, chapter 2 (3, in some editions), section 11. See Naftal, volume 2, pp. 84-85, for his proposed correction of the text in Pesachim 49a, which has Raban Gamliel in Yavneh instead of Lod at the time.
196. Sanhedrin 32b.
197. Eiruvin 35a; Rosh Hashanah 15a; Tosefta Mikvaos, chapter seven (eight) section 10; Yerushalmi Beitzah, chapter 3, section 2.
198. Tosefta Keilim, chapter 2.
199. Rosh Hashanah 31b.
200. Bava Metzia 59b.
201. Kiddushin 40a and Shabbos 29a.
202. Yuda Sheinfeld, *Vayar Menuchah* (Jerusalem: The Foundation for the Advancement of Torah Study, 2003) p. 134. See Tosefta Keilim, Bava Basra, chapter 2, section 3.
203. Tosefta Mikvaos, chapter seven (eight), section 11; Shabbos 29b; Sifrei, Devarim, Eikev, chapter 11, section 13; Sanhedrin 74a. See also Kiddushin 40b.
204. This is the opinion of Halevi, volume 1, chapter 25, from p. 362 forward. Naftal, volume 2, p. 90 agrees with him. However, other scholars have nominated Rabi Akiva or Rabi Yehoshua or Rabi Tarfon for that role. Raban Shimon ben Gamliel II did not become *Nasi* until after the failure of the Bar Kochba rebellion c.149 CE. See Naftal's footnote, p. 89.
205. Yevamos 122a.
206. This is the opinion of Halevi above.
207. See Midrash Eichah Rabasi, chapter 3, sections 5 and 10.
208. Philo estimated the total at over a million souls.
209. See Tosefta Arachin, chapter 2, sections 3 and 4; Tosefta Yoma (Yom HaKippurim) chapter 2, sections 5 and 6.
210. Succah 51b.

211. Philo estimates the Jewish population in Alexandria at that time at over 200,000 souls.
212. In 40 CE, 67 CE.
213. Succah 51b. The slaughter of hundreds of thousands of Jews recorded there is attributed in our text of that Talmudic passage to Alexander the Great. However, almost all scholars agree that Alexander is a euphemism for Trajan and his successor, Hadrian. See Gittin 57b, where Hadrian's name is clearly mentioned in association with the destruction of Alexandrian Jewry. The collective tragic events of 115-117 CE are called in Talmudic literature *Pulmos shel Kitos*—the War of Kitos, named for the Roman general who led the massacre of the Jews in Mesopotamia and later in the Land of Israel.
214. See Yerushalmi Succah, chapter 5, section 1, regarding the "river of blood" reaching Cyprus.
215. Taanis 18b. However, see Bereshis Rabah, chapter 64, section 8, where they are mentioned as being the leaders of Israel during the beginning years of Hadrian's reign, after the time of Quietus and Trajan.
216. Chapter 2, section 7.
217. Bereshis Rabah, chapter 64, section 8.
218. Ibid. Halevi (p. 575) is of the opinion that the complaints to Rome regarding the rebuilding of the Temple came from the Hellenists living in the Land of Israel and Egypt. There is also a theory that the early Christians were involved in sending false information to Hadrian. Since the Christians maintained that the loss of Jewish sovereignty in the Land of Israel and the destruction of the Temple were punishment for the rejection of Jesus by the Jews, it naturally follows that any restoration of Jewish sovereignty or rebuilding of the Temple would be theologically most problematic to them.
219. The Roman city built upon the place and ruins of Shomron, the ancient capital of the northern kingdom of Israel in First Temple times.
220. Ibid. Bereshis Rabah.
221. Ibid. See the famous universal parable about the stork removing the bone lodged in the lion's throat—and how the stork should be grateful for the mere fact of being able to extricate its head from the mouth of the lion!
222. Rosh Hashanah 31b.
223. Chulin 55b.
224. These decrees promulgated at Usha were not in the nature of new innovations, but rather came to reassert and strengthen decisions of the rabbis of previous generations. See Yerushalmi Peah, chapter 1, section 1 and in the *Pnei Moshe* commentary thereupon for an example of this type of law that had been forgotten and was now restored by the rabbis at Usha. See also Halevi, volume 1, chapter 25, p. 574.
225. Naftal, volume 1, p. 132, quoting Dio Cassius.
226. Ibid. See Bava Basra 60b.
227. Yevamos 16a. See also the commentary *Mitzpeh Eisan* to Yevamos 16a, where the commentator points out that the numerical value (*gematria*) of the Hebrew letters that comprise the phrase "from one end of the world to the other end" is 564 and that this is the exact number of times that Rabi Akiva's name is mentioned in the Talmud! However, see Konovitz, p. 10, for variant counts as to the number of times that Rabi Akiva is mentioned in the Mishnah and Talmud.
228. His famous statement was that loving one's friend as one's self is the great rule of the Torah. Bereshis Rabah, chapter 24, section 8.
229. Menachos 29b.

230. Sifrei, Zos HaBrachah.
231. Semachos 9a. The passage there may also be interpreted in such a way as to make his father, Yosef, the actual convert.
232. Ibid.
233. Konovitz, *Rabi Akiva* (Jerusalem: Mosad Harav Kook, 1965), pp. 12-16; Sheinfeld, chapter 10, based on Halevi.
234. The Talmud tells us that he was an unlettered person even at the age of 40. However, Halevi, Konovitz, Naftal and others are of the opinion that the Talmud did not mean that literally, but that when the Talmud says "forty years" its intent is to indicate a long time. All of the dates regarding Rabi Akiva's life and death are approximate, since different sources and scholars all offer different dates. The approximate date given here is a consensus compromise of all of the differing opinions.
235. Kesubos 62b.
236. Pesachim 49b.
237. Kesubos 62b; Nedarim 50a. Avos D'Rabi Nosson, chapter 6, section 2, has him beginning the study of Torah by sitting in the same class as his small son. Also see there that Rabi Akiva supported himself during his years of study by selling cords of wood.
238. Chagigah 12a.
239. Nedarim 50a.
240. Sheinfeld, p. 159, based on Halevi. See Konovitz, pp. 14-15, for a different opinion.
241. See note 233 above.
242. Nedarim 50a.
243. Kesubos 63a.
244. Nedarim 50a-b lists six different sources of his wealth. For a description of his great wealth see Avos D'Rabi Nosson, chapter 6, section 2; Shabbos 59b; Yerushalmi Sotah, chapter 9, section 16.
245. Eiruvin 86a.
246. Yerushalmi Maaser Sheini, chapter 5, section 4. See also Rashi, Kiddushin 27a.
247. Vayikra Rabah, chapter 34, section 15; Kallah Rabasi, chapter 2.
248. Avodah Zarah 10b. See Nedarim 50a-b and also there in Avodah Zarah that Rabi Akiva returned half of the money to Ketia's children and kept half for himself.
249. Bamidbar Rabah, chapter 9, section 27.
250. Rashi on Bechoros 58a; Rashbam, Pesachim 112a. That is why his son, Rabi Yehoshua, was called "ben Korcha," i.e. "son of the bald one."
251. See Haggadah shel Pesach, where his hosting the Seder in Bnei Brak for the scholars is recorded.
252. Yevamos 62b.
253. See Rashi, Koheles 12:3.
254. Sanhedrin 86a and Rashi there.
255. Avos D'Rabi Nosson, chapter 18.
256. Sanhedrin 86a.
257. Metaphorical comments on the Bible intended to communicate values and guidance in life, usually delivered in a story form.
258. Chagigah 14a.
259. Yerushalmi Berachos, chapter 1, section 1. Shteinman, in volume 2, p. 34, places his own allegorical interpretation to the dispute between Rabi Akiva and his colleagues regarding Aggadah. He maintains that in reality this was a discussion between them regarding the wisdom of supporting Bar Kochba's rebellion

against Rome.
260. Ibid.
261. Eiruvin 46b.
262. Berachos 36a.
263. Kiddushin 66b.
264. Taanis 25b. Rabi Akiva is the founder of the *Avinu Malkeinu* prayer.
265. Ibid.
266. See Berachos 60b; Makkos 24a-b.
267. Pesachim 112a; Yerushalmi Berachos, chapter 6, section 8.
268. Kesubos 63a and see Tosefos there.
269. Shabbos 147a.
270. Moed Katan 21b; Semachos, chapter 8.
271. Semachos, chapter 8.
272. Rosh Hashanah 26a.
273. Koheles Rabah, chapter 11, section 1.
274. Yerushalmi Horayos, chapter 3, section 7.
275. Ruth Rabah, chapter 6, section 2.
276. Avodah Zarah 34a.
277. Yevamos 98a.
278. Yevamos 121a.
279. Nedarim 50b.
280. Ibid. See the commentary of the Ran (Rabi Nissim ben Reuven, fifteenth century Spain) there.
281. A detailed description of the Bar Kochba rebellion may be found in my book, *Echoes of Glory* (Brooklyn, NY: Mesorah Press, 1995), chapter 12, p. 195 onward.
282. Yerushalmi Taanis, chapter 4, section 2.
283. Ibid.
284. Sanhedrin 97b.
285. Gittin 57a.
286. Ibid.
287. See Makkos 24a-b; Sanhedrin 101a.
288. Berachos 61b.
289. Ibid.
290. Megillas Taanis, at the conclusion of the last section of the book, states that Rabi Akiva was imprisoned on the fifth day of Tishrei, between Rosh Hashanah and Yom Kippur.
291. Eiruvin 21b; Pesachim 112a; Yevamos 108b.
292. Yevamos 62a.
293. Makkos 24a-b.
294. Berachos 61b.
295. Ibid.
296. Ibid.
297. Midrash, Mishlei, chapter 9; Yalkut Shimoni, volume 2, p. 944; Tosfos Bava Metzia 114a.
298. Ibid.

Section III

1. Moed Katan 26a; Terumos, chapter 10; Kesubos 8a.
2. Yerushalmi Chagigah, chapter 1, section 7; Yerushalmi Megillah, chapter 3, section 3.
3. Mechilta, Yisro, chapter 6; Shir HaShirim Rabah, chapter 2, section 18.
4. Though the martyrs are generally lumped together as the "Ten Martyrs," there were many more than ten scholars killed over a period of time. The ten martyrs listed in the prayer on Yom Kippur and Tisha B'av span almost a century in time.
5. Yerushalmi Chagigah, chapter 2, section 1; Bereshis Rabah, chapter 82, section 9.
6. See Avraham Moshe Naftal, HaTalmud V'yotzrav, volume 1 (Tel Aviv: Yavneh Publishing House, 1972), p. 146.
7. Shir Hashirim Rabah, chapter 2, section 18.
8. Sanhedrin 14a.
9. This opinion obviously holds that Rabi Meir and Rabi Nechemiah were two different persons. This is very likely true, as Rabi Nechemiah is quoted very often in the Talmud, where his opinion is obviously not in agreement with that of Rabi Meir. However, see Shabbos 147b, where there is an indication that Rabi Nechemiah is really Rabi Nehoray—who in turn is really Rabi Meir! Rabbi Reuven Margoliyus, in his Margoliyos HaYam, Sanhedrin, 86a, note one, states that Rabi Meir's real name was Rabi Nechemiah, but that there are many other scholars in the Talmud and Mishnah also named Rabi Nechemiah. Therefore, the Talmud did not mean to imply that every Rabi Nechemiah mentioned in the Mishnah is Rabi Meir.
10. Yerushalmi Sanhedrin, chapter 1, section 2; also see Yevamos 62b.
11. Sanhedrin 14a.
12. Ibid.
13. Yitzchak Isaac Halevi in Doros HaRishonim (Warsaw, 1896), section 1, volume 5, pp. 674 forward. Naftal, volume 1, pp. 147-149 follows Halevi's thesis as being correct.
14. There is disagreement amongst the scholars as to the identity of the "Antoninus" who was the friend of Rabi Yehudah HaNasi. There are those who say that he was the emperor Antoninus Pius. Others say that a later emperor, Marcus Aurelius Antoninus Pius, was the friend. Most historians are of this second opinion.
15. Yerushalmi Chagigah, chapter 3, section 1.
16. Shir HaShirim Rabah, chapter 2, section 16.
17. Meilah 17a. For a number of incisive statements of Rabi Reuven ben Eetzrebuli, see Avos D'Rabi Nosson, chapter 16, section 3; Moed Katan 18b.
18. Meilah 17a-b.
19. An enigmatic and sinister figure, mentioned only once more in the Talmud, Moed Katan, 9a-b. There, too, he plays a strange role regarding a curse/blessing given to the son of Rabi Shimon bar Yochai. See Shabbos, 33b and 34a, where it is written that he was "killed" by a glance from Rabi Shimon bar Yochai after the latter emerged from hiding.
20. Yerushalmi Sheviis, chapter 9, section 1.
21. Shabbos 33b.
22. Berachos 63b.
23. Bereshis Rabah, chapter 76, section 7.

24. Berachos 48b.
25. Naftal, pp.161-162.
26. Rosh Hashanah 31b.
27. See Eiruvin 13 b. "It is apparent to He Who created the world that there is no scholar in our generation equal to Rabi Meir…" Rabi Akiva chose Rabi Meir to be the Chacham ahead of Rabi Shimon bar Yochai. Rabi Shimon was hurt by this, but Rabi Akiva consoled him by saying: "Is it not sufficient for you that I and the Lord are aware of your powers?" See Yerushalmi Sanhedrin, chapter 1, section 2.
28. Horayos 13b.
29. Niddah 24b.
30. Gittin 56a.
31. Ibid.
32. Eiruvin 13b. His student, Sumchos, apparently resembled his mentor in this respect. He could declare any item to be impure or pure, with numerous reasons advanced for each position. See Eiruvin 13b; Yerushalmi Sanhedrin, chapter 4, section 1; Yalkut Shimoni Tehillim, section 658.
33. Gittin 67a; Eiruvin 13a; Koheles Rabah, chapter 2, section 22.
34. Eiruvin 13a.
35. Shabbos 134a; Yerushalmi Berachos, chapter 1, section 1.
36. Yerushalmi Moed Katan, chapter 3, section 1.
37. Ibid.
38. Beitzah 25b.
39. Pesachim 62b.
40. Avodah Zarah 18a.
41. Semachos 12a. See Shteinman, Be'er HaTalmud (Tel Aviv: Masada Press, 1967), volume 2, p. 71, for the opinion that the brother in question was a zealous nationalist—this was the *tarbus raah* referred to in the passage. He fought against the Romans and was killed by them.
42. Avodah Zarah 18a-b.
43. Ibid. The other reason given there in the Talmud as to why Rabi Meir fled will be discussed later in this section.
44. Yevamos 121a.
45. Ibid.
46. Brachos 10a; Eiruvin 53b and 54a.
47. Ibid. Eiruvin.
48. Pesachim 62b.
49. Yerushalmi Tosefta Keilim, Bava Kama, chapter 4, section 9; also see Tosefta Keilim, Bava Metzia, chapter 1, section 3, where she disputes Rabi Tarfon's opinion as well as those of other rabbis, and Rabi Yeshoshua [Yehudah] adopts her view as correct.
50. Shteinman, volume 2, p. 60 derives this from Avodah Zarah 18a. However, the Vilna edition of the text of that piece of the Talmud seems to refer not to Bruriah herself, but rather to the beauty of Bruriah's sister who was held captive by the Romans for immoral purposes.
51. Yalkut Shimoni, section 964.
52. Avodah Zarah 18b and Rashi there.
53. See his work Chibur Yafeh M'Hayeshua.
54. Yerushalmi Kilayim, chapter 9, section 3 (in some editions, 6).
55. Shteinman, volume 2, p. 60.
56. Avodah Zarah 18a.
57. Horayos 13b.

58. The subject was Uktzin, a complicated and technical matter dealing with the laws of purity regarding stems of fruits and other such types of materials.
59. Rabi Meir felt himself disqualified as Nasi due to his background of being descended from converts.
60. Horayos 14a.
61. Eiruvin 13b.
62. Horayos 14a.
63. Sanhedrin 86a.
64. Chagigah 15b.
65. Koheles Rabah, chapter 2, section 22.
66. Nazir 49b and 50a.
67. Chulin 142a; Kiddushin 39b.
68. Chagigah 15a.
69. Yerushalmi Chagigah, chapter 2, section 1.
70. Ibid. See Naftal, volume 2, p. 45, who quotes a variant text in that Yerushalmi which specifically mentions Acher acting as a Roman agent to betray scholars and religious Jews.
71. Chagigah 15b.
72. Ibid.
73. Ibid.
74. See Maharsha, Horayos 14a as to why Rabi Meir was called *acheirim*—plural, and not *acher*, singular.
75. For an example from our own time, see Naftal, volume 2, p. 144, who portrays Acher as a Roman collaborator and a traitor to Judaism and the Jewish people. On the other hand, Shteinman, volume 2, pp. 166-168, paints a much more sympathetic picture of him.
76. Avos, chapter 4, mishnah 26.
77. Moed Katan 20a.
78. Chagigah 15b.
79. Shabbos 25b.
80. Pesachim 49b.
81. Kiddushin 82a.
82. Sotah 35a.
83. Avos, chapter 4, mishnah 25.
84. Koheles Rabah, chapter 5, section 21.
85. Berachos 17a.
86. Bereshis Rabah, chapter 20, section 29. In the Torah text the word "ohr" describing the material of the clothes that God fashioned for Adam and Chava, is spelled with the first letter being an ayin, thus signifying leather, animal hides. Rabi Meir, however, spelled "ohr" with the first letter being an aleph, thereby signifying light.
87. Sifrei, Haazinu, chapter 32, section 5.
88. Berachos 10a.
89. Koheles Rabah, chapter 1, section 28.
90. Yalkut Shimoni Shir HaShirim, section 985; Avos D'Rabi Nosson, chapter 36, section 1.
91. Yevamos 48b.
92. Sifrei, Haazinu, chapter 32, section 43.
93. Sifrei, Zos HaBrachah, chapter 34, section 5. In the medieval manuscripts of this Midrash, Rabi Meir is identified as the author of this interpretation. Also, in Rashi's commentary to the Torah, Devarim 34:5, this idea is quoted in the name of Rabi Meir.

94. Yalkut Shimoni Melachim Aleph, section 201.
95. This great scholar was Rabi Meir's closest colleague and their discussions fill the pages of the Talmud. He was a person who lived in poverty, so much so that the Talmud in Nedarim 49b records that he and his wife had to share an outer cloak, so that both of them could never be outside of their house at the same time. His opinions in halachah were definitive in most of the Mishnah, and after the death of Rabi Meir, he was considered the head of the main yeshivah in the Land of Israel.
96. See Shabbos 118b that he fathered five sons who were all great scholars. Their names were Yishmael, Elazar, Chalafta, Avtilas and Menachem, and they are all mentioned as scholars in the Talmud.
97. After emerging from hiding from the Romans for thirteen years and returning to society, he found it difficult to adjust to the mundane world about him. Due to his own stellar level of holiness, he held his fellow humans to a very high standard of behavior and attitude. See Shabbos 33b. Tradition ascribes to him authorship of the basic work of kabbalah, the Zohar, though the book in its current form was not published until the fifteenth century. He is the Rabi Shimon most often and regularly quoted in the Mishnah.
98. He is the Rabi Elazar mentioned throughout the Mishnah (see Rashi, Shabbos 19b). The Romans executed him at the time of Hadrian's decrees.
99. Rabi Akiva's son.
100. One of the main and vociferous supporters of Raban Shimon ben Gamliel II in defeating Rabi Meir's and Rabi Nosson's attempt to depose him as Nasi.
101. Rambam, in his introduction to Mishneh Torah, lists him as a member of the beis din—the rabbinical court of Rabi. Hence, he could be considered a Tanna with great halachic authority. However, Rashi, in Niddah 18b, states authoritatively that he was an Amora, a member of the generation after Rabi, with lesser halachic authority than a Tanna.
102. Gittin 75a.
103. Yerushalmi Bava Basra, chapter 10, section 8.
104. See Nedarim 66b, where he allowed himself to be spat upon (!) in order to save a woman from her husband's foolish vow. See also Sanhedrin 10b, where Raban Shimon is seen as being much more humble and forthcoming in dealing with the other scholars than was his father, Raban Gamliel of Yavneh. See also the statement of his son, Rabi Yehudah HaNasi, in Bava Metzia 84b, about his father's great humility and self-effacement.
105. Sotah 46b.
106. Sifrei, Devarim 1:28.
107. Avodah Zarah 36a.
108. Bava Basra 133b.
109. Shabbos 130a. See also Sifrei, Devarim 1:2, where he makes the same statement regarding those commandments that Jews willingly risked their lives to fulfill.
110. Shabbos 128a.
111. Sotah 49b.
112. Rosh Hashanah 19a. See Naftal, volume 2, p. 172, where he places the events mentioned there in the Talmud as occurring shortly after the death of Raban Shimon ben Gamliel II. His conclusion is based on the opinion of Halevi, Doros HaRishonim, section 1, volume 5, p. 809 forward.
113. c.161—c.181 CE.
114. Apparently, there was another scholar who also was called Rabi, for in Yerushalmi Peah, chapter 1, section 5, there is a halachic discussion recorded

between "Rabi" and Rabi Yehudah HaNasi. Nevertheless, whenever the name Rabi appears in Mishnah or Talmud, one may generally assume that it refers to Rabi Yehudah HaNasi.

115. See Shabbos 118b that Rabi Yehudah HaNasi never placed his hand below his waist belt. There is a famous quip of Rabbi Meir Shapiro of Lublin (died 1933) that he knew many wealthy men—potential philanthropists turned misers—who unfortunately emulated this trait of Rabi Yehudah HaNasi of not putting their hands below their belts to reach for their wallets.

116. Tzipori and Beis Shearim, both located in the Lower Galilee. See Sanhedrin 32b.

117. This is the opinion of Rambam in his Introduction to Mishneh Torah, Rav Shmuel HaNagid in his Mavo LaTalmud, Rav Saadia Gaon and Rabbi Yeshayahu Di Trani (Tosfos Rid) commenting on Gittin 60a. See also Beitzah 2b and Bava Metzia 86a, which also indicate Rabi as actually completing and writing the Mishnah. However, in the introduction to Smag (Sefer Mitzvos Gadol, by Rabbi Moshe of Coucy) and in his commentary to Hilchos Shabbos, Mitzvah Lo Saaseh 65, it may be inferred that the Mishnah was written down in later generations after Rabi. See the article of Rabbi Y. Ben Tzvi in Mishpacha magazine, Shavuos 5766 issue. See also Rabbi Reuven Margoliyus' discussions in his book, Yesod HaMishnah V'Arichasa. I have followed the opinion of Rambam in the later text of this chapter.

118. Bava Basra, 5a.

119. See note 121 below.

120. See Naftal, volume 2, pp. 175-176 and 178.

121. See Shteinman, volume 2, p. 246. See Tosfos Avodah Zarah 10b that Antoninus was nursed as an infant by the mother of Rabi.

122. See Iggeres Rav Sherira Gaon, Levin edition, p. 21, where he states: "In the days of Rabi, the rabbis were freed from all evil decrees (shmad) because of the friendship that existed between Antoninus [As mentioned above, I have assumed throughout this book that the Talmud's Antoninus is Marcus Aurelius. BW] and Rabi and therefore they were able to agree on deciding all matters of halachah." Rav Sherira Gaon was the leader of Babylonian Jewry in the tenth century and wrote a concise history of Israel and its Torah tradition called Iggeres Rav Sherira Gaon: this "letter" has been reprinted many times and translated into many languages, including English.

123. Berachos 57b.

124. Yerushalmi Megillah, chapter 3, section 2.

125. Yerushalmi Sanhedrin, chapter 10, section 5; Megillah, chapter 3, section 2.

126. Yerushalmi Megillah, chapter 3, section 2.

127. Avodah Zarah 10b; Midrash Rabah Vayikra, chapter 3, section 2.

128. Yerushalmi Megillah, chapter 1, section 11; Yerushalmi Kilayim, chapter 9, section 3; Bereshis Rabah, chapter 34, section 12, chapter 75, section 3, chapter 84, section 1; Sanhedrin 91a; Avodah Zarah 10a-b, 11a-b and many other places in Talmud and Midrash.

129. Avodah Zarah 10a.

130. Berachos 16b.

131. Ibid.

132. Avodah Zarah 10b.

133. Avodah Zarah 11a. In the ancient world, before the advent of refrigeration and air cargo, having fresh vegetables on one's table year-round, even out of season, was the hallmark of true wealth.

134. Avodah Zarah 10b.

135. Gittin 59a.
136. Shabbos 113b
137. Shabbos 113b.
138. Chulin 7a.
139. Chulin 7b.
140. Chapter 6, sections 8 and 9.
141. The other six qualities, besides wealth, listed in the Mishnah are beauty of appearance, physical strength, honor, wisdom, old age and children.
142. Avos, chapter 6, mishnah 9.
143. See Rashi at Eiruvin.
144. Eiruvin 86a.
145. Bava Basra 8a.
146. Yerushalmi Chagigah, chapter 2, section 1.
147. Yevamos 121b.
148. Bava Metzia 84b.
149. Ibid.
150. Midrash Rabah, Bereshis, chapter 96, section 9.
151. Ibid.
152. Yerushalmi Pesachim, chapter 10, section 1.
153. Rashi, Succah 53a.
154. Succah 53a records that Levi would juggle and perform acrobatic acts to entertain Rabi.
155. Nedarim 50b.
156. Kesubos 104a.
157. Bava Metzia 85a. See also Yerushalmi Kilayim, chapter 9, section 3, where Rabi attempts to save the lives of the two sons of Rabi Reuven ben Eetzrebuli.
158. Bava Metzia 84b; Yerushalmi Shabbos, chapter 10, section 5.
159. Bava Metzia 84b.
160. Tosefta Oholos, chapter 5, section 10.
161. Bava Metzia 85b.
162. Ibid.
163. Ibid.
164. Nedarim 41a.
165. Yerushalmi Kilayim, chapter 9, section 3.
166. Yevamos 105b; Yerushalmi Kesubos, chapter 12, section 3.
167. Throughout the Talmud Bavli, he appears as simply Levi.
168. Yerushalmi Yevamos, chapter 12, section 6.
169. A great scholar and somewhat enigmatic figure. His troubling dreams were interpreted for him by Rabi in a favorable fashion. See Berachos 56b. He brought Rabi to laughter against Rabi's will. See Nedarim 51a. He preached the value of peace above all else. He summed up all of the Torah with the verse "Know God in all of your ways and He will straighten your path in life." See Berachos 63a. He was the one who informed the people of Tzipori of Rabi's death in an indirect and compassionate manner. See Yerushalmi Kilayim, chapter 9, section 3. He is mentioned as one of the three scholars whose teachings provide the student with all that he could wish for. See Yerushalmi Horayos, chapter 3, section 5. Nevertheless, he was an exacting teacher. See Berachos 39a and Krisus 8a.
170. This extraordinary individual had the power to restore Torah to Israel, even if all other Jews forgot it. See Bava Metzia 85b. Rabi Chiya was the uncle of Rav. See Sanhedrin 5a.
171. He was the father of Mar Shmuel and is usually referred to in the Talmud as

THE ORAL LAW OF SINAI

Abuha d'Shmuel, the father of Shmuel, and not by his given name.

172. He and Rabi Chiya are the first and main editors of the braisos—statements of halachah and tradition that preceded the writing of the Mishnah or that explain, modify or expand on the words of the Mishnah itself.

173. Rambam counts him as a member of Rabi's rabbinical court. Hence, he is considered a Tanna in terms of halachic authority. See Rambam's introduction to Mishneh Torah. He was one of Rabi's premier students and established a yeshivah of his own in the Upper Galilee, in the town of Achbari, after the death of Rabi. See Yerushalmi Eiruvin, chapter 8, section 4. Halevi casts him as the main teacher of Rabi Yochanan. See Doros HaRishonim, section 2, p. 273, etc. He was an extremely affluent person. See Bava Basra 14a. He supported the students who attended his yeshivah, and they in turn devoted part of their time and efforts to work on his properties and manage his enterprises. Regarding this, see Avodah Zarah 62b; Yerushalmi Sheviis, chapter 8, section 6; Yerushalmi Kiddushin, chapter 1, at the end of section 4.

174. A younger colleague of Rav. See Chulin 54a. While Rav left for Babylonia after the death of Rabi, Rabi Yochanan remained in the Land of Israel and became the founding head of the yeshivah in Tiberias. He is also the founding editor of Talmud Yerushalmi and one of the great Amoraim of that first generation after the completion of the Mishnah. He was one of the younger students at the time of Rabi's yeshivah.

175. A former gladiator and highwayman, he repented and became Rabi Yochanan's lifelong colleague. See Bava Metzia 84a. His life and achievements, as well as those of Rabi Yochanan, will be discussed more fully in the second section of this book series which will concern itself with the compilation and editing of the Talmud Bavli and Yerushalmi.

176. Niddah 62b.
177. Nedarim 41a.
178. Yerushalmi Bava Metzia, chapter 5, section 6.
179. Bava Kama 99a; Yerushalmi Bava Metzia, chapter 6, section 1.
180. Chulin 86a.
181. Bava Metzia 85b.
182. Ibid.
183. Midrash Rabah, Rus, chapter 3, section 4. See Shabbos 35a, where he says that the miraculous well of Miriam that accompanied the Jewish people in their wanderings in the Sinai desert can be seen amidst the waters of the Kineret (Sea of Galilee), which abuts Tiberias.
184. Yerushalmi Kesubos, chapter 12, section 3. See also Kiddushin 33a regarding Rabi Chiya's concentration on Torah: he did not even notice who passed before him.
185. Megillah 24b. Any American immigrant to Israel today is aware of this same failure.
186. Midrash Rabah, Bereshis, chapter 96, section 9.
187. Yerushalmi Kilayim, chapter 9, section 3.
188. Ibid.
189. Berachos 14a.
190. Shabbos 6b; Bava Metzia 92a.
191. Derech Eretz Zuta, chapter 7.
192. Midrash Rabah, Devarim, chapter 4, section 8.
193. Midrash Rabah, Esther, introduction.
194. Bava Metzia 85b.

195. Niddah 27a.
196. See Rashi, Chulin 106a.
197. Eiruvin 50b.
198. Berachos 18b.
199. Yerushalmi Shabbos, chapter 7, section 2.
200. Midrash Rabah, Vayikra, chapter 9, section 9.
201. Megillah 5b.
202. Rabi lived there for seventeen years. See Midrash Rabah, Bereshis, chapter 96, section 9. Rabi compared his seventeen years in Tzipori to the seventeen years that Yaakov spent in Egypt. Apparently, he felt it to be an exile, albeit a pleasant one.
203. Sanhedrin 32b.
204. Gittin 60b.
205. See Rashi there in Gittin that the prohibition against writing the Oral Law applies only when and if there is no danger that the Torah will be forgotten. See also Rashi, Berachos 54a, where he states: "There are times that we may ignore the words of the Torah in order to achieve an act for the sake of God . . . and then [we are allowed] to do something which apparently appears to be forbidden."
206. Rashi, Bava Metzia 33b.
207. It is not farfetched to see these words as an explanation, justification and defense of Rambam's own writing and publication of Mishneh Torah, his own remarkable compendium of all Jewish law and tradition—a work of scope such as had not been seen since Mishnaic and Talmudic times a thousand years earlier.
208. Levin edition, p. 21. See note 121 above.
209. Tamid 32b. Literally, he said, "he who foresees what will be born."
210. Bava Basra 12a.
211. Avodah Zarah 10a.
212. Ibid.
213. Avos, chapter 6, mishnah 1.
214. Known by its acronym, Shas. In common usage, this acronym is used to refer to the Talmud as well as the Mishnah.
215. Shabbos 31a. See also Midrash Shochar Tov, chapter 19, where the six orders of the Mishnah are based on a verse in Psalms, 19:7. The order of the six sedarim there is also different than the accepted order adopted by the Talmud in Shabbos 31a. See also Baal HaTurim commentary to the Torah, Devarim 26:17, where Rabbi Yaakov ben Asher bases the six orders of the Mishnah on that verse in the Torah itself.
216. Berachos, Peah, Demai, Kilayim, Sheviis, Terumos, Maasros, Maaser Sheni, Challah, Orlah and Bikurim.
217. Shabbos, Eiruvin, Pesachim, Shekalim, Yoma, Succah, Beitzah, Rosh Hashanah, Taanis, Megillah, Moed Katan and Chagigah.
218. Yevamos, Kesubos, Nedarim, Nazir, Sotah, Gittin, Kiddushin.
219. Bava Kama, Bava Metzia, Bava Basra, Sanhedrin, Makkos, Shvuos, Eduyos, Avodah Zarah, Avos, Horayos. Originally, Bava Kama, Bava Metzia and Bava Basra were considered one tractate. However, due to the volume of material in them, it was soon separated into three tractates. See Bava Kama 102a. Rambam, in his Commentary to the Mishnah, counts Bava Kama, Bava Metzia and Bava Basra as one tractate, as per that statement of the Talmud in Bava Kama 102a.
220. Zevachim, Menachos, Chulin, Bechoros, Arachin, T'murah, Krisus, Meilah,

THE ORAL LAW OF SINAI

Tamid, Midos and Kinim.

221. Keilim (because of its great length of 30 chapters was also sometimes divided into three sections, Bava Kama, Bava Metzia and Bava Basra, as was Nezikin. However, unlike Nezikin, Keilim always appears in our printed editions of the Mishnah as one tractate. Nevertheless in Tosefta, it appears as three tractates), Oholos, Negaim, Parah, Taharos, Mikvaos, Niddah, Machshirin, Zavim, Tvul Yom, Yadayim, Uktzin.

222. According to Rambam in note 219 above, there are only 61 tractates to the Mishnah.

223. See also Tosfos, Shabbos 81b and Avoda Zarah 22a where it is implied that there is no specific order of different tractates in the same seder of Mishnah.

224. These inferences being the basis for Rav Sherira Gaon's understanding that there is no order to the tractates.

225. Margoliyus, Yesod HaMishnah V'arichasa, p. 27 onwards. See there notes 6, 7, 8 and onwards. See also there his opinion that, originally, there were only five sedarim of Mishnah and Rabi eventually added a sixth (Zeraim). See also his opinion that Rabi was even of the opinion that ultimately there are seven sedarim—one dealing with the daily rituals and commandments incumbent upon a Jew to fulfill—but that his colleagues disagreed and Rabi therefore combined two of them (by, for instance, placing tractate Berachos in seder Zeraim, etc.) so that in the final version of Mishnah there are six sedarim.

226. Ibid. See especially pp. 29-30.
227. See Margoliyus, beginning on page 70.
228. Ibid., pp. 60-61.
229. Margoliyus, pp. 57-58.
230. Yevamos 30a.
231. Margoliyus p. 63.
232. Sanhedrin 86a.
233. Margoliyus, p. 64.
234. Ibid., p. 61.
235. "Who established the Mishnah?—Rabi!" Yevamos 64b.
236. Ibid.
237. For example, Berachos 13b.
238. For example, see Bava Kama 6b, where the Talmud explains that the Mishnah quoted the words of an earlier Tanna from Jerusalem exactly, even though that Tanna spoke in a manner that was "short."
239. See Yerushalmi Nazir, chapter 1, section 1.
240. Much of the vocabulary of modern Hebrew, as spoken in Israel, is taken from the Mishnah. This is especially true regarding the naming of fruits, vegetables, grains, tools, utensils, trades and locations.
241. Devarim 31:19.
242. Sifra, Bamidbar, Shlach.
243. See Margoliyus, p.36.
244. Midrash Rabah, Vayikra, chapter 21, section 5.
245. Sifrei, Devarim, Shoftim, chapter 17, section 19.
246. Bava Basra 154b. In Yerushalmi Horayos, chapter 3, section 5, Bar Kapara's breisos are called *mishnayos gedolos*—great mishnayos.
247. As mentioned above in note 166, he is usually referred to in the Talmud as simply Levi. His editions of breisos are mentioned in Yoma 24a and Yevamos 10a. See also Bava Basra 52b and in Rashbam there.
248. These two scholars authored and compiled the most authoritative and accepted

of all of the works of the breisos. See Chulin 141a-b that "any breisa that did not originate from the works of Rabi Chiya and Rabi Oshiya is suspect and should not be introduced into the study hall."
249. Yerushalmi Bava Kama, chapter 4, section 6; Kiddushin, chapter 1, section 3.
250. Naftal, pp. 183-184, detects two different trends of the scholars towards the breisos and their relationship to the study of Mishnah. One is to concentrate on the Mishnah itself—its wording and inferences—and pretty much to disregard the breisos, except where they help elucidate the Mishnah. He attributes this method to the school of Rabi Chanina bar Chama, mentioned above as being one of the main students of Rabi himself. The second school of thought—which is the one that the Talmud adopted in the main—always attempted to compare, and if possible reconcile, the decisions and wording of the Mishnah to the teachings of the breisos, sometimes even favoring the position of the breisa over that of the Mishnah. Margoliyus, p. 65, points out that even though the breisos are sometimes referred to as Mishnah they were never treated as really being Mishnah. See Rashbam, Bava Basra 138a, where he states that the word mishnaseinu, when it appears in the Talmud, always refers to the Mishnah of Rabi, while the word mishnah may sometimes really refer to a breisa.
251. Sanhedrin 86a. See also Yerushalmi Shabbos, chapter 8, section 1.
252. Margoliyus, p. 65.
253. Ibid.
254. Rabi and his sons were trained for leadership and communication with the Roman world. They were fastidious in manner, using mirrors to adjust their appearance, wore their hair in Roman style, and knew Greek language and culture. All of this was permitted to them because of the necessity of their representing Israel to the Roman authorities. See Yerushalmi Shabbos, chapter 6, section 1.
255. Shabbos 56a.
256. Avos D'Rabi Nosson, chapter 28.
257. Taanis 14b.
258. Sotah 49b.
259. Twice in seder Zeraim, three times in seder Moed, seven times in seder Nashim, five times in seder Nezikin, sixteen times in seder Kodashim, and only once in seder Taharos.
260. Kesuvos 103a-b.
261. Pesachim 112b.
262. Ibid. Naftal, p. 185, sees this appointment as being an honorary one, without much power attached to it. He also states that it was a controversial appointment to which the students of Rabi objected.
263. Sanhedrin 32b.
264. Yerushalmi Horayos, chapter 9, section 3.
265. Kesubos 103b.
266. Rashi Kesubos 104a.
267. Kesubos 103a-b.
268. Ibid.
269. Shteinman, volume 2, p. 121.
270. Kesubos 103a.
271. Kesubos 104a.
272. Ibid.
273. Ibid.
274. See Halevi, section 2, pp. 308-309; Zev Yavetz, Toldos Yisrael, volume 6 (Tel Aviv: Am Olam Publishers, 1963), p. 336; Gershon Alon, Mechkarim B'Toldos

275. Yisrael, volume 2, p. 322; and Naftal, p. 186, among other opinions.
275. Naftal, p.219.
276. Kiddushin 72b. In Midrash Rabah, Bereshis, chapter 58, section 1, it is stated that Rav Ada bar Ahava was born on the day of Rabi's death.
277. Raban Gamliel is quoted in Avos, chapter 2, mishnah 2; Shabbos 151b; Kesubos 10a; Sotah 15a; Menachos 84b; Chulin 8b, 98a, 106a, among other places. Rabi Shimon B'Rabi is mentioned tens of times in the Talmud. See for instance, Beitzah 28a; Kiddushin 22b; Shabbos 152b; Yevamos 105b and Chulin139b. He is mentioned in the Mishnah quoted in the Talmud in Makkos, chapter 3, 23b.
278. Avodah Zarah 19a; Yoma 87b; Kiddushin 33a.
279. Bava Basra 16b.
280. Yerushalmi Avodah Zarah, chapter 4, section 2.
281. Beitzah 28a.
282. Midrash Tanchuma, Bereshis, Vayeshev, section 3.
283. Ibid.
284. Megillah 24b. His voice was so unusual that if he were a kohein, it would have been considered a blemish, perhaps preventing him from blessing the people of Israel.
285. Kesubos 8a; Nedarim 50b.
286. Yerushalmi Shabbos, chapter 4, section 2.
287. Arachin 10a.
288. Ibid.
289. A group of quasi-Jews, the Samaritans, whose halachic status as Jews had been debated for centuries by the rabbis of the Mishnah. Eventually it became apparent that they still retained pagan practices, and it was for this reason that the more lenient view of them by the Mishnah was overturned by Raban Gamliel III.
290. Chulin 5a. See Rashi there who states: "Raban Gamliel [III] was the son of Rabi Yehudah HaNasi and he was of the last [of the Tannaim], and he and his court decided [to take a stricter view] on the matter of the *shechitah* done by *Kusim*, after our Mishnah had taught that it was permissible, and they now held it to be forbidden."
291. Avos, chapter 2, mishnah 2.
292. Pesachim 51a. See also Yerushalmi Shabbos, chapter 6, section 1, for a description of Raban Gamliel's slightly different behavior in a somewhat similar situation.
293. Ibid.
294. Avos, chapter 2, mishnah 2.
295. Tosefta, Sotah, chapter 6, section 8.
296. Kesubos 103b.
297. Shabbos 151b.
298. Ibid. Avos.
299. Sanhedrin 24a.

Glossary

Abuha D'Shmuel—the father of Mar Shmuel
Acharonim—the latter rabbinic scholars dating from the sixteenth century onwards
Acheirim—others
Acher—Rabi Elisha ben Avuyah—the "other" one—the apostate
Achnaee—a snake
Achsanya—an inn; a home
Aggadah—legend, metaphor, the non-halachic aspect and discipline of the Oral Law
Aggadic—referring to *aggadah*
Aleph—the first letter of the Hebrew alphabet.
Amidah—the basic eighteen (nineteen) blessing prayer recited thrice daily in Jewish prayer services
Amoraim—the scholars and authors of the Talmud
Apikores, Apikorsim—a non-believer, a rebel against Judaism's tenets and observances
Arvis—the evening/night prayer services
Oso hayom—that particular day, the day that Rabi Elazar ben Azaryah became the Nasi
Av beis din—the chief judge of a rabbinic court. In the times of the Sanhedrin, he was the assistant to the *Nasi*, who was the titular head of the Sanhedrin.
Avi Hamishna—literally, the "father" of the Mishnah. It was used in reference to *Rabi Oshiya*, the scholar most expert regarding the Mishnah
Avinu Malkeinu - a penitential prayer recited on fast days and the Ten Days of Repentance
Avos D'Rabi Nosson—an expanded form of the Mishnah tractate of Avos as developed in the yeshiva of Rabi Nosson in late Mishnaic times
Ayin Hara—the evil eye

Bas Kol—an "echo" from heaven, a spiritual message from heaven
Batei Din—Jewish rabbinic courts
Beis Din—a Jewish rabbinic court
Beis HaBechirah—a synonym for the Temple in Jerusalem; a commentary to the Talmud by Rabbi Menachem HaMeiri of fourteenth century Provence
Be'er HaTalmud—a four volume work by Eliezer Shteinman on the men of the Talmud
Beis HaVaad—literally, the meeting place of the scholars
Bikurim—the offering in the Temple of the first fruits of the yearly crop
Birkas HaMazon—the prayers that constitute grace after meals
Birchas HaMinin—the additional nineteenth blessing added to the Amidah. It is aimed to exclude proselytizing Jewish Christians from participating in Jewish prayer services and society

THE ORAL LAW OF SINAI

Bo Bayom—on that particular day
Breisa, Breisos—Talmudic comments and addenda to the Mishnah

C   *Chacham*—literally, a wise man. Also used as a rabbinic title.
Chatas—a sin offering in the Temple
Chaver—a Torah scholar; a friend
Chazara—a review session of the Talmudic lesson of the day
Cherem—a ban, to ostracize, excommunication
Ches—the eighth letter of the Hebrew alphabet
Chevra Kadisha—the holy society, a Jewish burial society
Chidush—a new original interpretation or explanation in Torah studies
Chilul Hashem—behavior that denigrates God's Name and Torah and Jews in the eyes of the public
Chulin—a tractate of Mishnah/Talmud; something which is not holy

D   *Darkei Noam*—ways of pleasantness. It is one of the basic values of Torah and Judaism.
Diaspora—the Jewish people scattered throughout the Exile in the world
Derech Eretz Zuta—a tractate of halacha and aggadah of immediate post-Talmudic times
Devarim—the fifth of the Five Books of Moses
Doros HaRishonim—a seminal Jewish history book written in the latter part of the nineteenth century by Yitzhak Isaac Halevi

E   *Eeseeyim*—Essenes, a sect of Jews that existed in Mishnaic times
Ein mazal l'Yisrael—literally Israel is not governed by any stars or constellations; it has also come to mean that Israel has no predetermined fortune; in the popular vernacular it is used to indicate that the Jewish people do not always have good luck.
Eiruv—literally, a mixing; an halachic construct that joins different properties positions as far as Sabbath and holiday requirements are concerned
Ells—a measure of distance
Eshkolos—Shehakol Bo—the combination of all positive qualities and talents in one person

G   *Gavrah Rabah*—a great person
Gavra Rabah U'mitla—a great man who limps
Gematria—the science of determining the numerical value of the letters of the Hebrew alphabet
Gemilus chasadim—acts of loving kindness and charity towards other human beings
Geonim—the rabbinic scholars and rulers of Jewish Babylonia from the seventh to the eleventh centuries
Giyura—a convert to Judaism

H   *Haggadah shel Pesach*—the book of the service of the Pesach seder
Halacha—Jewish Torah law and practice
Halacha l'Moshe miSinai—Jewish law and practice as received by Moses on Sinai, though not specifically mentioned or indicated in the text of the Torah itself
Halachos—specific Jewish Torah laws and practices
HaTalmud V'yotzrav—a multi-volume work by Avraham Naftal describing the history of the writing of the Mishnah and Talmud and sketching the lives of the scholars of that time
Hatzalah Poorta—a small salvation

Hilchos Melachim—the final section of Mishneh Torah authored by Rabbi Moshe ben Maimon

Iggeres Rav Sherira Gaon—a concise history of the Jewish people written by one of the leading scholars of tenth-century Babylonia

Kabbalah—the secret, hidden, spiritual, mystical interpretation of Torah and texts
Kabbalistic—relating to Kabbalah
Kapdan—someone who is exacting, a disciplinarian
Kareis—literally, "cut off." It refers to a heavenly punishment for sins by shortened life span.
Kesubah—the marriage contract between husband and wife detailing their obligations towards one another
Kidah—a form of bowing or prostrating one's self
Kiddush Hashem—behavior that sanctifies God's Name in the eyes of the public
Kodashim b'chutz—eating or slaughtering "holy" food from the sacrifices outside of the required Temple precincts
Kineret—the Sea of Galilee
Kinos—lamentations, dirges, prayers of sadness and mourning
Kodashim—the fifth series of the Mishnah dealing with laws of the Temple service and of kashrus
Kohein, kohanim—a member or members the priestly clan of Israel descended patrilineally from Aharon
Kohein Gadol—the great kohein, the High Priest of Israel
Koheles—the book of Ecclesiastes
Koreich—the "sandwich" of matzo, bitter herbs and the Paschal Lamb (in Temple times) eaten as part of the Pesach seder service
Knesses HaGedolah—the Great Assembly of 120 scholars convened and established at the time of Ezra and the beginning of the Second Temple times
Kusim—the Samaritans in Second Temple times. The word was later was used as a generic term for any and all non-Jews.

L'tarbus raah—joining a bad society, following a bad culture

Maasecha Yekarvucha, Umaasecha Yerachakucha—your actions and behavior will bring you closer to the scholars of Israel or they will distance you from them.
Maharsha—Rabbi Shmuel Eidelis, a sixteenth century Polish commentator to the Talmud
Maror—bitter herbs eaten as part of the Pesach seder service
Matzoh—the unleavened grain "bread" that is eaten by Jews on Pesach
Mavo LaTalmud—literally, The Introduction to the Talmud. A scholarly work written by Rabbi Shmuel Hanagid of eighth century Spain.
Mechadedei Tfei—sharper, more creative, more brilliant
Mechkarim B'Toldos Yisrael—a book of essays on matters of Jewish history
Megillos—literally, scrolls, manuscripts
Mesorah—literally, tradition. It is used especially regarding the punctuation and cantillation of the words of the Torah.
Midos—literally "measures." It is the name of a tractate in Mishnah. It also refers to human character traits.
Mincha—the afternoon prayer service
Minim—the early Christians; a synonym for Jewish apostates
Misah Yafah—a good death

THE ORAL LAW OF SINAI

Mishnah, Mishnayos—a section of Oral Law teachings as written and edited by Rabi Yehudah HaNasi of second/third century Galilee. The Mishnah is the basis for the Talmud.
Mishnah Rishona—the earliest forms of the Mishnah produced before the time of Rabi Yehudah HaNasi.
Mishnahso Kav V'Naki—his statements in the Mishnah are few in number but are of high quality
Mishneh Torah—the encyclopedic fourteen volume compilation of Rabbi Moshe ben Maimon (Rambam) of twelfth century Spain, Morocco and Egypt
Mitzvos—literally commandments. The 613 obligations of Jews as prescribed by the Torah.
Mitzpeh Eisan—a commentary to Talmud by a nineteenth century scholar, Rabbi Avraham Eisan
Moed—the second series of the Mishnah dealing with Sabbath and holidays
Mufla Sheb'sanhedrin—the most noted scholar sitting on the Sanhedrin
Musaf—the additional morning prayer on the New Moon, Sabbath and holidays
Mussar—ethics; chastisement

N *Nasi*—literally, prince, leader, president. The head of the Sanhedrin was the Nasi.
Nashim—the third series of the Mishnah dealing with domestic relations and vows
Nazir—a tractate of the Mishnah/Talmud; a person who has accepted Nazarite vows
Negaim—a volume of the Mishnah concerning the laws of purity regarding dermatological and other "plagues"
Nesi'im—the plural of nasi
Netzivin—a town in Babylonia, the home of Rabi Yehudah ben Bseira
Nezikin—the fourth series of the Mishnah dealing with matters of commerce, law, courts and torts

O *Oholos*—a volume of the Mishnah concerning the laws of purity and impurity regarding the presence of a corpse or its limbs in an enclosed area

P *Pardes*—literally, an orchard. It is a term euphemistically used to describe the place where one enters into deeply spiritual and metaphysical inquiry and thought.
Perush HaRambam l'Mishnah—the commentary of Maimonides to Mishnah
Perushim—the Pharisees; the group that composed the Tannaim of the Mishnah
Pnei Moshe—a commentary to Talmud Yerushalmi by Rabbi Moshe Margoliyus of seventeenth century Amsterdam and later of Lithuania
Pruzbul—a legalism created by Hillel to enable creditors to preserve their loans after the Sabbatical year passed
Pulmos Shel Kitos - the wars and persecution inflicted on the Jews by Kitos (Quietos) a Roman general

R *Rishonim*—the great rabbinic scholars of the Medieval Era
Rosh Yeshiva—the head of the yeshiva
Ruach HaKodesh—holy spirit, Divine inspiration

S *Stam Mishnah*—a Mishnah which has no attribution as to its author
Shochet—a ritual slaughterer of poultry and animals
Seder—one of the six orders of the Mishnah; the Pesach service and meal of the first night of the holiday

Seder Eliyahu Zuta—a minor tractate supplementing the Talmud from post-Talmudic times
Selichos—penitential prayers
Semichah—rabbinic ordination
Shacharis—the morning prayer service
Shechinah—the Divine Presence and Spirit
Shechitah—the ritual method of slaughtering animals and birds
Sh'Ein Tocho K'Varo—insincerity, hypocrisy
Shemittah—the sabbatical year occurring once every seven years
Sheyarei Knesses HaGedolah—the last surviving members of the Men of the Great Assembly constituted by Ezra
Shisha Sidrei Mishnah—the six orders of the Mishnah that comprises its entire content
Shma Yisrael—Hear O Israel. It is the basic declaration of the Judaic faith and testifies to God's oneness, unity and uniqueness It is recited twice daily by Jews in their prayer services.
Shmad—forced conversion, extermination
Shmoneh Esrei—literally, eighteen. It is the name commonly used for the standing part of the three prayer services of the day. It contains eighteen blessings, hence its name. A nineteenth blessing was added in Mishnaic times but the name "eighteen" remained in popular use.
Simchas Beis HaShoevah—the celebration in Jerusalem on *Succos* in honor of the drawing of the water for the libation of the water on the altar of the Temple
Stam Mishnah Rabi Meir—a Mishnah that has no author attributed to it in its text is from Rabi Meir
Succah—the booth in which Jews reside during the festival of *Succos*
Succos—the plural of succah

T

Taharos—the sixth series of the Mishnah dealing with the laws of ritual purity
Tahor—hebrew word for "pure"
Takanos - rabbinic ordinances
Takanos Usha—the decrees and decisions of the Sanhedrin when it met in Usha
Tanna Hu uPalig - he is a Tanna and therefore can disagree with the opinion of the Mishnah
Tannaim—the scholars of the Mishnah
Targum or *Tirgum*—the translation of the Torah into a non-Hebrew language, usually Aramaic or Greek
Tefillin—phylacteries
Teshuva—repentance
Tikun haolam—perfecting the world
Tosefta—a collection of braysos that complement the Talmud arranged in a separate work
Tzaddik—a most righteous, holy person
Tzedokim—the Sadducees
Tzipor—bird

U

Uktzin—the final tractate of the Mishnah

V

Vatran—someone who gives up on one's rights easily, a forgiving person
Vayikrah Rabah—the section of Midrash Rabah dealing with Vayikra/Leviticus

W

World to Come—spiritual afterlife after physical death; the world after the messianic era

Y   *Yalkut Shimoni*—an anthology of aggadic interpretations of the Torah by the medieval sage, Rabbi Shimon Hadarshan
Yalkut Shimoni Tehillim—the Yalkut Shimoni to Psalms
Yatza L'Tarbus Raah—literally, went out to a bad environment or culture. It became an accepted euphuism for apostasy as well.
Yesh Omrim—there are those who say
Yesod HaMishnah v'Arichasa—a seminal work on the origins of the Mishnah by Rabbi Reuven Margoliyus, a noted twentieth century scholar
Yetzer Hara—the evil inclination within humans

Z   *Zecher L'Mikdash*—a reminder of the Temple and its rituals and procedures
Zechus—a merit
Zeir—hebrew for "small" or "little"
Zeraim—the first series of the Mishnah dealing with agricultural issues
Zohar - the basic book of kabbalistic thought attributed to Rabi Shimon ben Yochai of third century Land of Israel
Zugos—literally, pairs. The early Tannaim until Hillel and Shammai were paired together in their studies and teachings and positions in the Sanhedrin.

About the Author

Rabbi Berel Wein, the founder and director of The Destiny Foundation since 1996, has, for over 20 years, been identified with the popularization of Jewish history through worldwide lectures, his more than 600 audiotapes, books, seminars, educational tours and, most recently, dramatic and documentary films.

Rabbi Wein is a graduate of the Hebrew Theological College and Roosevelt College in Chicago. He received his Juris Doctor Degree from De Paul University Law School and a Doctor of Hebrew Letters from Hebrew Theological College.

Rabbi Wein was a practicing lawyer for a number of years and in 1964 assumed the pulpit of the Beth Israel Congregation in Miami Beach, Florida, where he remained until 1972. In 1973 he became the Rabbi of Congregation Bais Torah in Suffern, New York and remained in that position for 24 years. He was then appointed Executive Vice President of the Union of Orthodox Organizations of America and was Rabbinic Administrator of the Kashrus Division for five years after that.

In 1977 he founded Yeshiva Shaarei Torah in Suffern, New York and remained its Rosh Hayeshiva until 1997. Rabbi Wein's book of halachic essays, *Chikrei Halacha* was published by Mosad Harav Kook in 1976 and *Eyunim B'm'sechtoth Hatalmud* was published in 1989.

Rabbi Wein has authored four Jewish history books—*Triumph of Survival, The Story of the Jews in the Modern Era; Herald of Destiny, the Medieval Era; Echoes of Glory, the Classical Era* and *Faith and Fate, The story of the Jews in the Twentieth Century*—all of which have received popular and critical acclaim.

Rabbi Wein authors and edits a monthly newsletter—*The Wein Press*—a source of information and inspiration on topics of Jewish interest. He also pens a weekly column for *The Jerusalem Post.*

Currently, the Destiny Foundation is in the process of translating Rabbi Wein's riveting accounts of Jewish history into a series of films on Jewish personalities—the first, entitled *Rashi–A Light After The Dark Ages,* was released in 2000, and *Rambam–The Story of Maimonides* had its premiere in New York, in November 2004. Currently in production, The Destiny Foundation is preparing a 10-part documentary series, based on Rabbi Wein's history of the Jews in the twentieth century, *Faith & Fate.*

Rabbi Wein, a member of the Illinois Bar Association, received the Educator of the Year Award from The Covenant Foundation in 1993. Most recently, Rabbi Wein received the Torah Prize Award from Machon Harav Frank in Jerusalem for his achievements in teaching Torah and spreading Judaism throughout the world. Rabbi Wein and his wife now make their home in Jerusalem.

Index

A

Abba bar Abba *120, 125*
Abba Shaul ben Batnis *47, 54*
Abba Sikra *61*
Abuha d'Shmuel *169*
Achbari *169*
Acher *91, 108, 113-115, 165, 174*
Admon *47, 54*
Aelia Capitalina *92*
Akavya ben Mehalalel *47, 52*
Alexander the Great *15*
Alexander Yanai *23, 25, 26, 28, 29, 151*
Alexandria *15, 23, 24, 67, 87, 88, 160*
Antigonus *15, 17, 20, 31*
Antipater *29, 30, 33, 36, 99*
Antipras *99*
Antoninus *105, 121, 122, 130, 132, 141, 163, 167*
Antoninus Pius *105, 163*
Aristoblus *28, 151*
Arvis *80*
Av Beis Din *19, 20, 22, 23, 25, 33, 150, 152*
Avtalyon *VII, XXII, 25, 30, 31, 32, 33, 36*

B

Baba ben Buta *32, 41*
Bar Kapara *120, 125, 137, 141, 171*
Bar Kochba *4, 62, 92, 97, 98, 103, 107, 119, 159, 162*
Baruch ben Neriyah *12*
bas kol *38, 174*
Baysosim *17, 22*
Beis HaVaad *75*
Beis Shearim *128, 130, 139, 140, 167*
Beitar *97, 98, 103, 106*
Birchas HaMinin *48, 51*

Bnei Brak *94, 161*
Bnei Bseira *33, 34, 68, 152*
breisa *175*
breisos *137, 138, 171, 172*
Bror Chayil *58*
Bruriah *109, 110, 115, 164*

C

Caligula *67*
Chaggai *11*
Chanan *54*
Chanina (Chananya) Sgan HaKohanim *52*
cherem *72, 108, 109, 158, 175*
Chezkiyah *126, 127, 128*
chisurei mechsara *136*
Choni HaMaagel *25, 27, 55, 56*
Chonyo *15*
Christian *45, 48, 142*
Christianity *57, 88, 103, 142, 143*
Christians *33*
Constantine *143*
Cyrenaica *67, 88*

D

Domitian *83*
Dustai ish Kfar Yavneh *32, 41*

E

Egypt *12, 15, 23, 25, 177*
Essenes *33*
Ezra *VII, XXII, 4, 6, 11, 12-16, 21, 32, 37, 78, 81, 93, 150*

F

Flaccum *67, 157*

G

Galilee *31, 83, 84, 86, 87, 90, 105, 106, 107, 125, 128, 140, 167, 169, 176, 177*
Glass *20, 21*
Great Assembly *4, 6, 11, 13-16, 50, 135, 176. See also Knesses HaGedolah*

H

Hadrian *89, 90, 92, 97, 103, 104-106, 160, 166*
Hasmonean *19, 23- 25, 35*
Hellenist *18*
Herod *19, 30, 31, 33, 35, 39*
Herodian *33*
hidden megillos *19*
High Priest *12, 13, 26, 28, 150, 176. See also Kohein Gadol*

Hillel 6, 7, 22, 30-39, 41, 45-47, 49-51, 53, 55, 58, 63, 64, 68, 71, 76, 79-81, 90, 93, 94, 130, 135, 139, 150, 152-154, 158, 177, 179
House of Hillel 35, 50, 53
House of Shammai 35

J

Julius Lucius Quietus 88

K

Kalba Savua 93, 94
Knesses HaGedolah 11, 14, 19, 176
Kohein Gadol 11, 12, 15, 16, 150
Kusim 142, 173

L

Lod 58, 62, 72, 79, 86-88, 159
Lulianus 88

M

Malachi 11
Marcus Aurelius 118-121, 129, 163, 167
Mar Shmuel 174
Mattisyahu 23
Menachem 32-34, 38, 150, 152, 153
midos 34
Mishnah Rishonah 19
Mishneh Torah 131, 136, 166, 167, 169, 170
Mordechai 11
Moshe ben Maimon. *See Rambam*
mufla sheb'sanhedrin 46

N

Nachum HaMadi 54
Nasi 13, 19, 20, 22, 23, 25, 26, 33, 45-47, 49, 55, 64, 68, 78, 80, 87, 91, 107, 111, 116, 117, 120, 125, 132, 138-140, 142, 150, 152, 153, 157, 159, 166
Nehardea 177
Nerva 85, 86
Netzivin 177
Nitai HaArbeili 20, 23, 24, 25

O

Onkelos 48

P

Pappas 88
Peki'in 75
Perushim 19, 23, 25, 26, 28, 32, 39
Philo 67, 159, 160

Pompey *19, 29*

Q

Quietus *88, 89, 90, 160*

R

Raban Gamliel *VIII, XXIII, 45-55, 58, 62, 64, 66-73, 75-87, 91, 111, 117, 120, 125, 142, 153, 154, 157-159, 166, 173*
Raban Gamliel I *45-55, 58, 154*
Raban Gamliel III *120, 125, 142, 173*
Raban Shimon ben Gamliel *45-47, 53, 58, 73, 91, 107, 108, 110-112, 116-118, 120, 132, 159, 166*
Raban Shimon ben Gamliel II *73, 91, 107, 108, 110, 111, 112, 116-118, 120, 132, 159, 166*
Raban Shimon ben Hillel *VIII, XXIII, 32, 46, 47, 53*
Raban Yochanan ben Zakai *47, 53, 58, 59, 63, 66, 70, 71, 73, 75, 76, 93, 94, 141, 156, 157*
Rabi. *See Rabi Yehudah HaNasi*
Rabi Akiva *VIII, XXIII, 17, 54, 58, 62, 70, 73, 77, 81, 83, 85-87, 90-99, 104, 108, 109, 135, 156-162, 164, 166*
Rabi Chalafta *87*
Rabi Chananya ben Tradyon *87, 109*
Rabi Chanina (Chananya) Sgan HaKohanim *VIII, XXIII, 52*
Rabi Chanina bar Chama *139, 172*
Rabi Chanina ben Dosa *47*
Rabi Chanina Sgan HaKohanim *47*
Rabi Chiya *120, 123, 125-128, 137, 138, 141, 168, 169, 172*
Rabi Chutzpis HaMeturgaman *86*
Rabi Dosa *15, 17, 77, 78, 91-93, 150*
Rabi Dosa ben Hyrkanos *15, 17, 77, 91, 92*
Rabi Elazar ben Arach *58, 67, 68, 70, 73*
Rabi Elazar ben Azaryah *81, 82, 85-87, 95*
Rabi Elazar ben Parta *91*
Rabi Elazar ben Rabi Yosi *105*
Rabi Elazar ben Shamua *91, 98, 104, 108, 116*
Rabi Elazar ben Shimon *106, 108, 117, 120, 124, 125*
Rabi Elazar HaModai *97*
Rabi Eliezer ben Hyrkonos *VIII, XXIII, 67, 68, 70, 108*
Rabi Eliezer ben Yaakov *47, 53, 54, 157*
Rabi Elisha ben Avuyah (Acher) *113*
Rabi Levi ben Sissas *120, 125, 126, 137*
Rabi Meir *VIII, XXIII, 91, 94, 98, 104, 105, 107-117, 125, 135, 163-166, 178*
Rabi Menachem HaMeiri *134*
Rabi Myashia *47, 54*
Rabi Nechemiah *94, 104, 138, 163*
Rabi Nosson *91, 107, 108, 110-112, 116, 117, 120, 135, 155-158, 161, 163, 165, 166, 172, 174*
Rabi Nosson HaBavli *107*
Rabi Oshiya *120, 125, 138, 172*
Rabi Pinchas ben Yair *122*
Rabi Reuven ben Eetzrebuli *105, 163, 168*

Rabi Shimon bar Yochai *95, 98, 104-107, 116, 124, 125, 163, 164*
Rabi Shimon ben Nesanel *67*
Rabi Shimon ish HaMitzpah *54*
Rabi Tarfon *70, 81, 83, 86, 87, 91-95, 117, 120, 124, 159, 164*
Rabi Yaakov ben Korshai *116*
Rabi Yanai *120, 125*
Rabi Yehoshua ben Chananya *VIII, XXIII, 58, 66-68, 70, 73, 90, 91*
Rabi Yehoshua ben Korcha *91, 108, 116*
Rabi Yehoshua ben Levi *91, 108, 116*
Rabi Yehudah bar Eelai *91, 94, 98, 104, 113*
Rabi Yehudah ben Bseira *54*
Rabi Yehudah HaNasi *VIII, XXIII, 45, 112-114, 120, 152, 163, 167, 173*
Rabi Yesheivov *87, 91*
Rabi Yesheivov HaSofer *91*
Rabi Yishmael *34, 55, 73, 83, 87, 90-92, 108, 120, 135*
Rabi Yitzchak ben Avdimi *120, 126*
Rabi Yochanan *32, 65, 87, 91, 97, 106, 108, 114, 116, 120, 156, 157, 169*
Rabi Yochanan ben Nuri *87, 91*
Rabi Yochanan HaSandlar *116*
Rabi Yosei HaKohen *67*
Rabi Yossi *87, 91, 95, 104, 105, 108, 116, 117, 120, 125, 126*
Rabi Zadok *58, 62, 79*
Rabi Zadok min HaKohanim *41*
Rambam *17, 130-132, 134, 136, 166, 167, 169, 170, 171*
Rashi *110, 130, 132, 154, 161, 164, 165, 166, 168, 170, 172, 173*
Rav Abba bar Eyvu *125*
Rav Chanina bar Chama *125*
Rav Chiya *126*
Rav Levi ben Sissas *123*
Rav Sherira Gaon *132, 134, 167, 171*
Reish Lakish *125*
ruach hakodesh *51*

S

Sadducees *17, 18, 19, 24, 33, 178*
Samaritans *90, 142, 173*
Sanhedrin *13, 14, 21, 24-26, 30, 31, 33, 41, 46, 47-49, 52, 64, 65, 70, 72, 75, 77, 79, 83, 84, 85, 90, 91, 94, 104, 105, 107, 111, 112, 131, 140, 150-159, 161-168, 170-174, 177, 179*
Sebastia *90*
Second Temple *4, 15, 16, 19, 45, 51, 52, 53, 57, 58, 150, 176*
semichah *104, 178*
Shammai *VII, XXII, 6, 7, 22, 32-39, 41, 45, 71, 73, 79-81, 130, 135, 152, 153, 179*
Shavna *33*
Shfar'am *107*
Shimi *15*
Shimon ben Azai *91, 96*
Shimon ben Hillel *VIII, XXIII, 32, 45, 46, 47, 53*
Shimon ben Shetach *VII, XXII, 23, 25, 26, 27, 28, 30*
Shimon HaTzaddik *VII, XXII, 15, 16, 17, 21*
Shimon HaTzanua *54*

Shlomzion (Salome Alexandra) *25, 27, 28*
shmad *103, 167*
Shmaya *VII, XXII, 25, 30-33, 36*
Shmuel HaKatan *47, 48, 51, 154*
Sumchos *108, 120, 125, 164*

T

takanos *41, 64, 91, 178*
takanos Usha *91*
tekiasa d'bei Rav *178*
Ten Tribes *30*
Tiberias *84, 99, 110, 126-128, 169*
Tiberius Alexander *67*
Tinnaeus Rufus *97*
Todos Ish Romi *25, 27*
Tosefta *138, 171*
Trajan *86-89, 160*
Tzadok and Baysos *17, 20*
Tzedokim *17, 22, 24, 26, 28, 33, 63, 178*
Tzipori *86, 87, 106, 107, 128, 130, 139, 140, 167, 168, 170*

U

Usha *58, 62, 79, 83, 84-87, 90, 91, 94, 105, 106, 107, 160*

V

Vespasian *60-62, 84, 85*

Y

Yavneh *32, 41, 53, 55, 58, 60-62, 64-66, 68, 70,-73, 75, 76, 78, 82, 83, 86, 90, 91, 94, 105, 106, 107, 111, 120, 153, 154, 159, 163, 166*
Yehoshua ben Kapusai *91, 96*
Yehoshua ben Prachyah *VII, XXII, 23, 24, 151*
Yehudah ben Baba *104*
Yehudah ben Tabai *VII, XXII, 25, 26, 30*
Yehudah Hyrkan *28, 29, 151*
Yochanan Hyrkanos *23*
Yoezer ish Habirah *32, 41*
Yosi ben Yochanan *VII, XXII, 20, 21, 22*
Yosi ben Yoezer *VII, XXII, 20, 21, 22*

Z

Zealots *60, 61*
Zechariah *11*
Zecharyah ben Kavutal *54*
zecher l'Mikdash *68*
Zeirei I *126*
Zerubavel *11, 16*
Zugos *VII, XXII, 6, 17-26, 31, 32, 150*

Photo Credits

Cover	© Library of the Hungarian Academy of Sciences, Budapest
Page 2	© IMJ (Collection of the Israel Antiquities Authority)
Page 5	© The Trustees of the British Museum
Page 6	© The Gross Family Collection, Israel
Page 12	© 2008 Artists Rights Society (ARS), New York / ADAGP, Paris Courtesy of the Spaightwood Galleries, http://spaightwoodgalleries.com
Page 13	© IMJ (Collection of the Israel Antiquities Authority, by Yoram Lehman)
Page 14	© IMJ, by David Harris
Page 15	© IMJ
Page 16	© IMJ
Page 21	© IMJ
Page 27	© Bible Land Pictures Photo Archive
Pages 28-29	© Bible Land Pictures Photo Archive
Pages 30-31	© Bible Land Pictures Photo Archive
Page 35	© Yeshivat Tikun Hamidot, Kiryat Yam
Page 36	© Yeshivat Tikun Hamidot, Kiryat Yam
Page 40	© The University and State Library of Darmstadt
Page 44	© IMJ by Meidad Suchowolski

Page 47	© Bible Land Pictures Photo Archive
Page 48	© 2003 State Hermitage Museum
Page 50	© IMJ
Page 55	© Bible Land Pictures Photo Archive
Page 56	© IMJ (Collection of the Israel Antiquities Authority)
Page 61	© The Trustees of the British Museum
Page 62	© Bible Land Pictures Photo Archive
Page 69	© Bible Land Pictures Photo Archive
Page 71	© IMJ (Collection of the Israel Antiquities Authority)
Pages 74-75	© Bible Land Pictures Photo Archive
Page 89	© IMJ (Collection of the Israel Antiquities Authority)
Page 91	© Yeshivat Tikun Hamidot, Kiryat Yam
Page 92	© Bible Land Pictures Photo Archive
Page 95	© IMJ
Page 96	© IMJ (Collection of the Israel Antiquities Authority)
Page 98	© IMJ
Page 104	© Yeshivat Tikun Hamidot, Kiryat Yam
Page 107	© Yeshivat Tikun Hamidot, Kiryat Yam
Page 116	© Yeshivat Tikun Hamidot, Kiryat Yam
Page 118	© Bible Land Pictures Photo Archive
Page 123	© Yeshivat Tikun Hamidot, Kiryat Yam
Page 124	© Bible Land Pictures Photo Archive
Page 128	© Bible Land Pictures Photo Archive
Page 132	© IMJ
Page 137	© Bible Land Pictures Photo Archive (Courtesy of the Sepphoris Expedition, The Hebrew University of Jerusalem. Photo: G. Laron)
Page 142	© IMJ (Collection of the Israel Antiquities Authority)